Yang Tai Chi Chuan

JOHN HINE

Hine Tai Chi Schools

Published by Hine Tai Chi Schools Ltd
PO Box 159
Bromley
Kent
BR1 3XX

First edition 1992
Reprinted 1994, 1998, 2002, 2006

ISBN 0 9534920 0 1

A CIP catalogue record for this book
is available from the British Library.

Acknowledgements
All photography by Sylvio Dokov

Printed and bound in Great Britain by:
MPG Books Ltd, Bodmin, Cornwall

Contents

THE AUTHOR

John Hine has studied the martial arts and mental disciplines of the Far East since 1962. In that time he has trained under several fine masters and experts both in the UK and in the Far East. He began his Tai Chi training in 1972, and has studied with five Tai Chi teachers. Prominent among them was master K. H. Chu, one of the three heirs to the Yang Style of Tai Chi, who were taught by grand master Yang Shou Chung. Sifu Hine has also trained with Master L. H. Lo, a direct Tai Chi descendent of the famous Yang family, especially skilled in the use of Tai Chi weapons.

Prior to his instruction in Tai Chi, he had extensively trained in the martial arts, teaching Karate, Tae Kwon Do and Northern & Southern Chinese Boxing. His Chi Kung training formally began in 1968, with Master Chang Cheong Kung, who had spent his life travelling the Far East studying the martial arts; his knowledge was of the highest order. In addition John Hine is a Sifu in both Hsing - Yi and Pa Kua which he learned alongside Tai Chi; he still teaches both arts.

In keeping with tradition he is also a healer and spiritual teacher. His training in Chinese Medicine included Acupuncture, Dietary Therapy and Herbal Medicine. He is also a qualified Naturopath and holds a Diploma in Medical Science.

His spiritual training has encompassed both Eastern and Western Mysticism. Having become a Buddhist when he was seventeen, he has intensively studied and practised meditation and personal development ever since with several teachers. This led him to the disciplines of Psychology, Hypnosis, NLP and Autogenics, which he found reinforced and strengthened his spiritual training. He regularly lectures and holds seminars on Personal Development, Tai Chi and Health. John Hine is a respected media adviser, having worked with TV companies, and has featured extensively in the national press and many top magazines.

John Hine heads an extensive network of Schools in England and has numerous Students throughout the World and was a Founding Member of the All Styles Tai Chi Union for Great Britain. He is also a Registered Acupuncturist and Certified Hypnotherapist.

Hine Tai Chi Schools has produced a DVD of the Tai Chi Long Form as taught in this book. To order your copy of the DVD please either visit our website at www.taichi-europe.com or send a SAE or international reply coupon to:
Hine Tai Chi Schools, PO Box 159, Bromley, Kent, BR1 3XX, England

For information on forthcoming courses, seminars for Tai Chi, Pa Kua and Hsing Yi send an SAE, or international reply coupon to:-
Hine Tai Chi Schools, PO Box 159, Bromley, Kent, BR1 3XX, England

Preface

The popularity of tai chi is increasing at a rate faster than ever before. People in all walks of life are now profiting from its practice. The health benefits have attracted both young and old alike in ever increasing numbers. Yet tai chi is more than simply an art for health or gentle exercise; it is a way of life. Tai chi is meditation in movement, a martial art, and a whole new way of perceiving yourself and everything around you.

Yang style tai chi chuan is the most widely practised of all the types of tai chi. Many of the short versions of the art now proliferating are based upon the Yang style. But the short form gives only a fraction of the whole, and as such an unbalanced view of the complete art.

This volume should be viewed as a workbook, a practical tool to assist you onwards and upwards with your practice of tai chi. If you are currently studying with a teacher, it should help as a handy reference to that teaching, outside of the class. For those who are new to tai chi, without access to competent instruction, this book can serve as a practical guide with its step-by-step teaching.

Beyond the solo exercise, there are chapters on pushing hands (a two person exercise), meditation, *chi kung*, self-defence applications and, finally, the double-edged sword form.

Straight ward off (see page 94)

Introduction

The ever increasing numbers of people practising tai chi has created the need for a clear view of what tai chi is. Many misconceptions have grown up since its introduction to the West. It has been portrayed as 'dancing', or 'mysticism', or an art only for elderly people. All are incorrect. Tai chi has a depth and breadth which can appeal to all age groups and both sexes.

Due to the fact that, on occasion, tai chi has been taught piecemeal to certain interest groups, the public perception has been distorted. To many people a superficial knowledge of the solo exercise is all that is necessary before you can teach others the art. As such it has relegated tai chi to a mere 'exercise' and robbed it of the status of a truly great art.

Tai chi's impact on an individual can be immense, changing your view of yourself and everything around you. Tai chi solo exercise or 'form' has many levels of expertise. For those simply wishing to improve their health, correct practice of the basic level form will yield pleasing benefits. Increased vitality, improved general well-being and a sense of calmness are common reports from students. Greater benefits accrue as you progress to the higher levels of expertise. Increased spiritual awareness, flexibility and robust good health are the rewards.

A change in the way you react to situations will take place also. A calm enters your life and tense situations become less so. Such immense changes, however, do not come without some effort, and consistent practice is essential. Eventually, the ability to circulate *chi* (vital energy) freely around your body can be achieved, with accompanying improvements in health, both physical and mental. Abilities way beyond this are obtainable, but are outside the scope of this book and can be obtained only with personal guidance from a good teacher.

As great as the benefits are from practising the tai chi empty hand form, training with a partner has added advantages. Pushing hands - or *tui shou* - increases your ability to maintain calm while trying to cope with your partner's continuously changing actions. At a basic level there are set routines of pushing hands exercises. Partners push, parry and control one another's movements in a relaxed fashion, and attempt to put the lessons learned in the solo form into practice. Winning is not part of these 'fixed step' pushing hands exercises. Learning from doing is the aim. Once the rules for practice are explained, the students will run through the routine slowly, trying to sense what is happening. Touch is the dominant sense used for this purpose; with practice, deep, rapt concentration will follow. The intense but relaxed state is akin to meditation in movement, with a stillness of mind and a clarity of vision.

For those wishing to become expert in the martial arts applications of tai chi, pushing hands is the first essential step. Being able to control an assailant is a first prerequisite for self-defence. At the basic stage of pushing hands practice, many valuable lessons are learned. Once a student's skill is great enough, those with a competitive bent can take part in free-style pushing hands training. In a prescribed area (sizes vary) in which nothing other than the soles of the feet can touch the ground, each competitor attempts to push the other out of the area using their tai chi skill, not brute strength. Alternatively, each will attempt to throw the other to the ground. Hands or knees touching the ground will score a point for the training partner. It must be stressed that a good level of skill should have been attained before free-style pushing hands is attempted. To do otherwise leads to the use of brute strength and completely goes against the spirit of tai chi.

Hine Tai Chi Schools strongly endorses the use of a matted area on which to practise free-style *tui shou* to protect the students when they are thrown to the ground. Safety is the obvious priority. Consistent training in pushing hands will sharpen the reflexes and develop the skills necessary for effective self-defence. Again, it must be stressed that it is not compulsory to take part in competitive pushing hands training, but a knowledge of its practice will give you a clearer overall view on the subject.

Stilling the mind and attuning yourself to a higher awareness are the aims not only of meditation but also tai chi. Together they form a common alliance against the modern ills of stress, frustration and feelings of alienation. The meditation technique taught in this book could easily have been included in the chapter on *chi kung,* since it has energising properties as well. It is a well known and widely practised meditation for those seeking good health as well as a calm mind.

Chi kung or 'vital energy accumulation exercise' is used by both martial artists and health promoters. Literally hundreds of *chi kung* routines are practised in the Far East. Many are specific to either the martial arts or to health; some, however, are common to both. The routine detailed within this book is used by both martial artists and health-minded individuals alike. As such it will appeal to the widest possible audience.

Often when students begin to learn the tai chi solo form, they will express no interest in the self-defence applications. However, once they have progressed through the form their curiosity has been aroused as to what it all means. Tai chi's philosophy on self-defence is to use the other's strength and control their actions. *Tui shou* (pushing hands) teaches the ability to sense and control through touch. The solo form supplies the self-defence techniques, and the self-defence applications training teaches the footwork and overall use for practical application. Each attack is dealt with by either evading with the help of tai chi footwork, or lightly parrying the assault. At no time are forceful blocks applied. The obvious beneficiaries are the majority of the population, who are neither natural athletes nor physically able to be strong and athletic.

One of the abilities acquired with continued practice of pushing hands is that of 'sticking energy'. Constantly trying to sense your partner's movements during pushing practice leads to an intuitive feel for their actions. Whenever they move forwards you will mirror the action and retreat before them at exactly the same speed. When your partner is retreating you will still stick to him or her, following each action precisely. With a skilled and experienced individual, they appear to stick to you like glue and prove very difficult to evade. This may seem to be no more than an interesting phenomenon in a class setting. But, in an actual self-defence situation, once the tai chi exponent has stuck to you, he will quickly tie up your hands and strike, pressing home the attack with hands, feet and grappling manoeuvres. Consequently, the time spent practising pushing hands can be applied usefully beyond the benefits of a psycho-physical exercise.

To extend the skills and abilities gathered from the tai chi solo form requires the use of the tai chi weapons. It may seem odd to equate weapons training with an advance in your tai chi skills, but on closer examination it will become clear. The double-edged straight sword, for instance, creates a relatively awkward weight on the end of your arm. Trying to move with skill and grace at first is impossible, with what appears to be the bane of your life in your hand. Perseverance comes to the rescue; with consistent practice the dead implement comes to life in your hand. Movements flow and the sword becomes part of you; an alien implement turns into a servant of your will. The rationale is - you can extend your *chi* or vital energy to the tips of your fingers and toes. To make it flow stronger you must extend its effects beyond your body. To achieve this the tai chi swordsman directs the energy and the point of focus to the tip of the sword. Thus when you make the sword do what you will, and can focus your energy to the sword tip, you will have forced the *chi* to flow beyond its normal boundaries.

Following this logic, the longer the implement used, the greater the increase in internal strength used to apply. This explains the order in which the tai chi weapons are taught, with the double-edged straight sword (or broadsword) at the beginning, through to the lance. The broadsword, which is heavier than the double-edged sword, can be taught first or second in the tai chi syllabus, depending on the teacher. Each of the broadsword movements tends to be longer, with wide sweeping motions emphasised. Greater effort and concentration is required to perform the exercise with elegance and control.

The staff can be from six to in some cases 13ft (1.8-4m) long. At its shortest length it will be twice as long as either of the swords learned previously. But by the time you have progressed to this point, you will be used to extending your skills beyond your present capability.

The last weapon to learn is the lance, and although it is generally shorter than some of the staffs, it requires great skill to use well. The added requirement of skill is due to the nature of the wood used in its manufacture. There are two types - yellow rattan and white waxy wood. The chief characteristic of these two is that of flexibility, necessary when performing with the lance.

The body of the lance should bend and whip at the student's will, responding to the mental direction of the wielder. This gives the appearance akin to the actions of a snake, with the lance tip moving like the head of the reptile. The lance not only extends your vital energy, but also improves your physical condition, with the vigorous movements of the lance exercises.

The basic syllabus outlined above should give a much broader understanding of the wider skills available in tai chi training. Some of you will not wish to go beyond the tai chi solo form and improving your health, but the rest of the system is there waiting for you to change your mind and sample the greater benefits that can be achieved.

What is tai chi?

The tai chi form is a series of slow moving exercises, performed smoothly and accurately, with the muscles as relaxed as possible, and the mind absorbed in each movement.

Tai chi is practised by millions of people who consider it to be an integral part of their everyday lives, giving robust good health, a calm stress-free mind and a flexible body. Tai chi is not designed to promote muscle size or enhance physical endurance. It is used to stimulate the internal organs gently, exercise the body, calm the nervous system and mobilise the joints. With consistent correct practice, the tai chi form leaves you warm, relaxed and gently stimulated. In time the mind has a stillness and clarity rarely experienced with other forms of exercise. Calmness eventually pervades the whole body, leaving you less stressed and more refreshed at the end of the day.

The tai chi form is but a part of the whole tai chi chuan system. *Tai chi* means 'grand ultimate', which refers to the original Taoist beliefs of the origins of existence. *Chuan* can be translated literally as 'boxing'. Originally tai chi chuan was a formidable martial art which was also beneficial to health. Now the health aspect, in most schools, has taken over completely. Many students do not even realise that they are practising a martial art.

Apart from the slow tai chi form, at a more advanced stage the students are introduced to the fast form. Relaxation and gentleness are still used, but at a higher speed. With this training the student acquires stamina and nimbleness to add to the calmness.

Pushing hands practice for two people increases sensitivity and the ability to cope with changing situations, as the partners perform pre-set movements. The vast array of martial arts techniques at the disposal of the tai chi student gives a lifetime of potential study in this most excellent self-defence system.

San shou, or 'free hands' two-man fighting exercise, allows the students to combine their techniques into a flowing interchange with a partner, giving flexibility and dexterity in combat applications. Each person has a series of attack and counter-attack manoeuvres to learn, which you could call 'side A' and 'side B'. When side A and side B have completed their own attack-and-defence series against each other, they immediately move into the other's technique routine; that is, side A will then begin side B's series of attack and defence, and vice versa. The *san shou* then forms a complete loop, with continuous and unbroken activity on both sides. When the *san shou is* practised alone, sides A and B are strung together in a flowing form. If explosive force is then added to the *san shou* form, it is described as *pao chuan,* or 'exploding fist'. *Chi kung* (or vital energy accumulation exercise) is an integral part of traditional tai chi training, resulting in a healthier body, a calmer mind and strong self-defence power.

Chi

Chi can be freely translated as 'vital energy' or 'life force'. Every living thing in the universe is said to possess *chi*. It is that which gives us life, the vital spark which lets us live, move and function. When the term is applied specifically to human beings, it refers to the energy freely circulating around the body. This concept is shared by many cultures, notably the Indian Yogis, who call it *prana,* the Tibetan *tummo,* and the Japanese *ki.* In the West the notion of a circulating life force within the body is no longer fashionable but, in the past, it was a generally accepted idea and was widely ascribed to in the cures of Anton Mesmer. Prior to Mesmer the ancient Greeks referred to this energy as *pneuma.*

In Chinese medicine and *chi kung (chi* cultivation arts), *chi* is designated as a 'Yin' or insubstantial energy- it can be felt but has no obvious form, whereas the human body has form and is a gross energy that is classified as 'Yang'.

The ancient philosophy of Taoism divided everything in the universe as either 'Yin' or 'Yang', and the universal symbol represents that idea (fig. 1). Yin is anything which has a female quality - caring, yielding, softness, night, are examples of what may be described as Yin. Its symbolic colour is black. Yang is the exact opposite, representing male qualities of strength, aggression, hardness, day, and whose colour is white.

When *chi* is strong, the body is vibrant and active; when weak, the opposite occurs. In order to be strong and healthy, *chi* must be abundant and flowing smoothly.

Fig. 1 Universal Yin/Yang symbol

An explanation of how *chi* circulates is now in order. The body has 12 main channels or 'meridians', which function like rivers distributing *chi* throughout the body. There are eight extra channels whose function is to store and regulate the energy, and generally act as reservoirs. Each channel is connected to an organ and runs to a foot or hand, ending at the fingers or toes. The energy passes along the channel to nourish and give life to that organ, and on through the channels feeding the other organs. Between every one of the major routes there are a countless number of tiny tributaries or canals. These interconnect all of the main channels and supply *chi* to the skin.

When the *chi* is low, stagnating or blocked at a point, ill health and weakness will result. At this time one of three options could be used to rebalance the situation. An acupuncturist could diagnose the problem and insert needles at the appropriate points to regulate the energy flow. A herbalist could administer specific combinations of herbs after diagnosis. This would be to readjust the behaviour of the energy within the organ and the smooth flow of energy along the channel. In turn this would affect all of the channels through which the *chi* passes. The third method would be to practise one of the three internal exercises and martial arts of tai chi - *pa kua, hsing yi,* or *chi kung.* The combination of the movements, breathing and calm relaxation could restore the energy back to normal. The use of exercises such as these is usually as a *preventive* against ill health, rather than a cure. When the malfunction in the body has reached a critical point, medical treatment is usually called for to redress the balance. This is then followed by the exercise therapy to reinforce the treatment and maintain the return to balance.

The ageing process is also governed by the quality, strength and smooth flow of vital energy in the body. If the organs are not functioning at their peak, the body will never reach its potential, shortening the life-span of the individual. Until the early part of this century there were longevity schools in China, where old masters would train their followers with the aim of a vastly extended life expectancy. To reach the goal the internal martial arts, *chi kung* exercise, dietary control and the taking of specific herbs and extracts were followed. The results, apparently, could be spectacular, with schools full of centenarians in some instances. The students must have possessed a great deal of dogged determination to follow such a spartan regime, while also being able to afford the extremely expensive herbs and extracts required.

In the practice of acquiring *chi,* certain points of the body are of special interest. At these points *chi* can be regulated and strengthened. The most prominent is the *tan tien,* which is situated two inches below the navel. This is the hub of all tai chi activity, and the place where energy circulation starts and finishes. By building up energy at this point, the *chi* can be made to flow into the main meridians, and strengthen the body. Almost as important as the *tan tien* is *ming men* (or the 'life gate') which is situated on the spine in the small of the back. This is sometimes called the 'back *tan tien'* and is a very important point not only in *chi kung,* but also in acupuncture.

The major point in the foot is called *yong guan* ('bubbling well'), which is situated on the sole and is the starting point of the kidney meridian. The kidney *chi* plays a major role in the health of the body; being at the beginning of the channel is of great significance. At the other end of the body you will find the point called *bai hui*, which can be found on the top of the head. At this junction the energy flow of the head and the onward flow of energy can be controlled.

Chi and the martial arts

The mind controls the chi, the chi controls the strength. So runs the traditional law governing the use of *chi* in the internal martial arts. The body requires a minimum amount of vital energy for our daily lives. This you could call 'core energy'. Any extra energy is stored within the body and added to your potential strength. This internal strength can be trained and brought under the control of the mind.

The relationship of the mind and the *chi* is somewhat akin to a rider and a horse: the mind is the rider and the *chi* is the horse. Once the horse is trained it will go wherever the rider commands. After consistent, correct training, the accumulated *chi* can be led to any part of the body in a fraction of a second, by the mind. Thus when you are performing the tai chi form, pushing hands or self-defence applications, you first form the idea of doing something a split second before you do it. Instantly your energy will lead your body to perform the task required.

If you doubt this mind-body relationship, perform the following test. Try to walk forwards while you are thinking about standing still. You will find that you cannot move; all the actions of the body are governed by the mind. The mind forms the idea of the task you wish to accomplish, and the energy sends impulses to the muscles and tendons to move in a prescribed way. Thus, when you wish to deliver a powerful strike, you command the body to do so, sending a surge of force to the hand or foot. When *chi* is concentrated in this explosive form it is called *Jing (Ching)* or 'essence'.

The inter-relationship between the mind, body and *Jing* might be explained best with the analogy of a car. The *chi* you can think of as petrol, or the prime mover of the car- without it the vehicle could not run. The body of the car is the human body, with the wheels representing your arms and legs. The driver and the steering wheel represent your mind and the centre or *tan tien*. Wherever they direct, the car will follow. *Jing* is the momentum of the car, and the potential explosive force now inherent in it. Therefore *Jing* is the total force of the combination of *all* of the factors involved. *Chi* is not *Jing* - it is the prime mover which helps to create this explosive energy.

The three internal martial arts

Tai chi chuan

The chief characteristic of tai chi is a deep relaxation of the body, so that the *chi* can circulate freely. When the tai chi explosive force *(Jing)* is used it is soft like a whip, but with deep penetrating power. Tai chi strategy in fighting is defensive, preferring to wait for the opponent to attack, and then using the oncoming force against the attacker. A strategy such as this enables even elderly tai chi practitioners to overcome a much younger assailant, not by contending strength against strength, but by using the mind allied to their skill and experience. All defensive movements are circular in nature. The tai chi defender endeavours to 'stick' to the attacker by using the acute sense of touch acquired through training.

Tai chi has a large array of kicks, but tends to use them to support the hands in self-defence applications. At close quarters tai chi commands an extensive array of throwing and grappling manoeuvres.

Hsing yi

Hsing yi requires that you be relaxed and natural. When both defending and attacking the movement is relaxed until the last instant, when the body stiffens momentarily as the *hsing yi Jing* is emitted. *Hsing yi Jing* is like a piece of bamboo, flexible but possessing shocking force. This force is characterised as being heavy like a cannon ball.

Hsing yi fighting strategy is much more assertive than that of tai chi - direct in its actions and preferring to move offensively as a form of defence, instantly countering every attack with one of its own, frequently at the same time. The mind and body move as one with a consistent forward momentum, hence the art's name 'mind fist'. Dodging, slipping and side-stepping are also used at a higher level. The 'mind fist' possesses several kicks, but tends to keep them low and blend them with an explosive barrage from the hands.

The basic arsenal of the various *hsing yi* styles encompasses the use of straight and circular punches, palm strikes, elbow, shoulder, head butt, kicking both high and low, and throwing and grappling.

Pa kua chang

The movements of *pa kua* are not as forceful as *hsing yi* or as soft as tai chi. Spiralling and whip-like power emanate from *pa kua* techniques. Always circular in appearance, its footwork is lightning fast, complex and evasive, patterned on the imaginary movements of a dragon. (The dragon was thought to be as light as a bird, with the elusive quality of a snake.) More defensive than *hsing yi,* a circular defence is quickly followed by a powerful circular attack with one of a vast array of hand, foot or body attacks, or throws. *Pa kua* strategy is to move to the side or rear of an opponent and attack the aggressor in their most vulnerable position. Throwing manoeuvres are used extensively, while striking techniques are aimed at vital points.

    Pa kua has many kicking manoeuvres hidden within the *pa kua chang* form (72 in total). Occasionally kicks are aimed at the head, usually when the attacker least expects it and with lightning speed.

    Pa kua chang literally means 'eight diagrams palm' and is aligned with the ancient Taoist philosophy of the *I Ching (Yi Jing)* or 'Book of Changes'. The basis of this philosophy is the dynamic inter-connections between all things in existence, both animate and inanimate. The basic eight manoeuvres of *pa kua chang* can be ascribed to the eight core trigrams of the *Yi Ching*. These eight trigrams are considered as the prime movers in existence, which in turn have eight actions each, making 64 actions. These 64 have also eight actions, and so on. It is a mathematical philosophy of great complexity which attempts to place Man and his actions in context with the cosmos.

The history of tai chi chuan

There are many theories as to the origins of tai chi chuan. Many schools believe the founder was the Taoist monk Chan San Feng, who lived in the Sung Dynasty (AD 960-1279). The legend states that Chan San Feng watched a battle between a snake and a bird ten times its size. As the bird lunged at its prey, the wily reptile dodged and weaved, lashing back at its tormentor with relaxed lightning speed. Eventually the exhausted bird flew off for easier prey. In that instant the art of tai chi was said to have been born.

Chan San Feng, a master of the hard Shaolin martial arts, applied the principles he had witnessed in the actions of the snake to his martial arts expertise. The snake's actions exemplified the Taoist principles of softness, relaxation, flexibility and naturalness, allied to the ancient breathing exercises to stimulate *chi* development.

It is not until the seventeenth century that tai chi can be verified historically. Henen Province in northern China was home to the Chen family of tai chi. This family has been credited with developing the Chen style, from which all the major schools - directly or indirectly - have developed. It is generally accepted that this 'new' style of martial art was developed from the popular existing arts at the time. The difference was that its movements were soft and it did not *contend* with opponents: adapting to the movements and yielding were its hallmark.

The legendary story as to the origin of Yang tai chi claims that at the beginning of the nineteenth century, Chen Chan Sheng headed the Chen family tai chi, which at the time was taught secretly to family members only. A young man by the name of Yang Lu Chan wished desperately to learn the art of the Chens'. Knowing that he would be refused if he asked to study with them, he became a servant in the household. He watched secretly as they trained at night, and during his free periods he would imitate the techniques he had seen. One fateful evening he was caught spying on the Chens. When he was ordered to vie against the family members, he managed to throw his adversaries to the ground. Chen Chan Sheng was so impressed that he immediately offered to teach Yang as if he were a family member.

Yang Lu Chan eventually left the Chens and returned home, where he spread the art of tai chi chuan far and wide. Yang's skill became known to the imperial Royal

Family, who are said to have ordered him to secrecy. He was admonished to teach only the Royal Family the art, and to keep it secret from the commoners. Yang did not do this, but passed on the art to many students in secrecy.

Yang Lu Chan had two sons - Yang Pan Hou and Yang Chien Hou.

Yang Pan Hou was the elder. He had an irritable disposition and did not bear fools lightly. His special skill was his apparent ability to 'stick' to his opponents, making it almost impossible to shake his light but tenacious hold. Pan Hou was a man of such great skill that he eventually taught the Imperial Guard.

Yang Chien Hou was the exact opposite of his elder brother. Gentle in nature, he would refuse all challenges to fight, not wishing to cause harm to others for personal gain. But that does not mean he could not fight; his tai chi skill was of the highest order, as was his teaching ability. He was said to be virtually unbeatable in the tai chi sport of free-style pushing hands. Even into old age, young men could not match his immense pushing skill.

In free-style pushing hands, two people vie against each other and attempt to use their skill to either push the other out of the area, or throw them to the ground. One young master at the time reported going to a free-style pushing hands event where the winner of one contest would stay in the area and take on the next. When he arrived an old man with a long, wispy beard was standing in the middle of the area. One young opponent after another was hurled out of the ring with apparent ease. On seeing this the young man came to the conclusion that the others were apparently not very good and he would have to show them how it was done. After all, this old man did not look much! Within seconds of stepping into the area, the young man was catapulted out with great force. Much chastened, he paid his respects to the old man he now knew was Yang Chien Hou.

In their youth, Yang Lu Chan was an uncompromising teacher who pushed his two sons hard. Quite often the boys would receive split lips during training. Such were the conditions that Pan Hou ran away; but he was caught and returned home. Chien Hou actually tried to hang himself, but was prevented from doing so by other members of the household. Eventually, Yang Lu Chan relented and slackened his harsh regime.

Yang Shou Hou was the eldest son of Chien Hou. He was said to have been brilliant in the skills of tai chi. His outstanding ability was the 'small frame' tai chi form of the Yang style. In the small frame form, each of the movements is small and compact compared with the other more expansive versions of the art. One of his famous students was *hsing yi* master Wang Hsiang Chai.

Yang Cheng Fu followed in his father Chien Hou's footsteps by leading the Yang family. Cheng Fu is famous for his modification of the old Yang form into the most widely practised style of tai chi today, taught in this book. All Yang tai chi forms prior to Yang Cheng Fu are now described as 'Old'. Cheng Fu removed the explosive strikes and flying kicks, and created the smooth, expansive movements now associated with the Yang style. Yang Cheng Fu was an extremely large man with prodigious strength, and trained six hours a day. Standing six feet (1.8m) tall and weighing 280lbs (127kg), he was a formidable figure with some of the character traits of his uncle Yang Pan Hou.

Yang Cheng Fu had three sons, two of whom stayed on in China. The eldest son, Yang Shou Chung, took over his father's mantle and moved to Hong Kong where he headed the international Tai Chi Chuan Association. After a long and distinguished career teaching many excellent students and spreading the art beyond the Far East, he died at the age of 93. One of his three leading students was master Chu King Hung. Upon the death of Yang Shou Chung, Chu, along with his two fellow disciples, took up the mantle as leaders of the international Tai Chi Chuan Association.

Prior to training with Yang Shou Chung, Chu King Hung had studied under master Fu Wing Fei of Canton. Fu Wing Fei was not only famous for his skill in tai chi, but also in the internal arts of *hsing yi* and *pa kua.* Allied to his tai chi skill, Chu King Hung also studied with *hsing yi/pa kua* Grand Master Hon Sing Woon and attained great skill in these arts. Chu King Hung eventually moved to the West where, among others, he passed on his knowledge and skills to the author.

During Yang Cheng Fu's extensive teaching tours, he was assisted by his nephew Fu Jong Wen. Fu was Yang Cheng Fu's right-hand man, and very gifted in the art of tai chi. He is currently one of the most respected Yang style tai chi masters in China.

Tai chi and health

The value of tai chi chuan as a therapeutic exercise has been known for hundreds of years, but it is only in recent years that scientific research has validated what was known intuitively.

Extensive comparative studies have been carried out using tai chi. One such study involved two groups of a similar age. Measurements were taken for physical strength, respiratory efficiency, circulatory function and skeletal strength. Group A were taught tai chi and instructed to practise every day. Group B, on the other hand, were left to go about their normal lives. At the end of the study the two groups were compared again in the above categories. Group A (the tai chi group) were considerably stronger physically, and in every other respect by a large margin, than the other, non-training group.

In China a vast amount of research has been carried out into the effects of tai chi and *chi kung* on various physical and mental conditions. The results vary from good to quite extraordinary in many instances. Set out below are some of the effects found on the human body that are due to tai chi practice.

Cerebral cortex/nervous system

(The cerebral cortex is the principal controller of both mental and physical function in Man.) The tai chi form harmonises the movements of the four limbs (with the head and torso) and causes a state of calm. This harmonisation engenders great tranquillity and the total relaxation of the muscles. The whole nervous system is relaxed and stress no longer has its disastrous effects. Perception becomes clearer and the nervous impulses to the organs run smoothly and efficiently. With constant practice, this 'anti-stress effect' lasts the day through. It is known that stress causes many degenerative diseases, including heart disease, cancer and arthritis. Therefore, tai chi's action can benefit numerous physical functions and be an important medical preventive.

Muscular/skeletal system

Tai chi's gentleness, the slowness of movements and the holding of the correct posture, make the muscles work gently and thoroughly. It gives tone and strength, without the side effects of more vigorous exercise. The joints are similarly exercised and strengthened during practice. Gentle pressure and constant motion mobilise the articulations, which helps to free their action, even into old age.

Posture improves measurably, and the skeletal system functions correctly, enhancing bodily health and one's perception of oneself. Tendons which control flexibility are gently stretched, and the tell tale signs of age are minimised.

Circulatory system

The American Heart Association advises that you should exercise and achieve 60% of your M.H.R. (Maximum Heart Rate). In experiments in the United States, the research volunteers achieved this level of heart rate by using low level tai chi stances during the form, but without the excessive strain of running and similar exercise. Thus, a beneficial effect can be obtained for people wishing to exercise the heart, to keep it healthy without the bump and grind of standard exercise routines.

The form exercises the vascular system and research has shown that it causes vasodilation (increase in the diameter of blood vessels), thus increasing blood flow in the body. It has been noted that the skin is helped in this respect, consistent practice of the overall action of the form helping to smooth and tone.

Respiratory system

Diaphragmatic breathing deepens the action of the lungs and helps oxygenate the system, stimulating vitality and helping to remove unwanted bodily toxins. The functions of both the respiratory and circulatory systems are enhanced by the free flow and efficient oxygenation of the blood. This helps the brain to work at peak efficiency.

Incorrect breathing has been associated with several degenerative diseases - when you consider that the average person uses less than one third of the lungs' capacity, insufficient oxygenation would seem the obvious conclusion. A deeper breathing pattern has also been found to affect the lymphatic system which removes toxic waste from the body. Unlike the circulatory system, which has the heart, the lymphatic system has no pump to move the lymph around the body. The increased breathing volume assists in this respect.

Digestive system

The diaphragmatic breathing and circular motions of the form massage the organs, including those of the digestive system, aiding their functions. The lack of stress on the nervous system and the correct nerve function to the digestive organs benefit the whole system. This has prompted tai chi's use in Far Eastern hospitals specialising in ulcers of the digestive tract, with quite impressive results.

With greater efficiency of the digestive organs, increased benefit can be achieved from the food taken in, enhancing the general well-being of the body. When the mind is agitated and under stress, more acid is secreted into the stomach. If the acid is allowed to become too strong, an ulcer will form, either in the stomach or the small intestine. With a calm mind, the excess acid will cease to over-produce, and the body will be assisted in healing the ulcer. The alleviation of stress is obviously a very important adjunct to medical professionals treating digestive complaints.

Glandular system

Due to the posture and movements of tai chi, the glandular system is toned and exercised. The glandular system plays an intrinsic role in the proper functioning of the internal organs. Without glandular participation, none of the major organs would function correctly.

The glandular system controls all aspects of the sexual system. Sexual reproduction and the physical male and female characteristics during adolescence are instigated by these glands. The menstrual cycle in women is also directly controlled by the glandular system.

The immune response is triggered within the body from the activities of the glands and their associated organs.

Metabolism

Metabolism is controlled by the glandular system and the metabolic rate. The metabolic rate is the speed at which energy, and consequently bodily fat, is burned in the body.

Tai chi exercise aids in the control of metabolism and thus helps to normalise body weight. Several other functions are also said to be enhanced by regular tai chi practice.

Immune system

It is believed that internal exercise affects the functioning of the thymus gland, which is closely related to the immune system. The thymus plays an active role in the production of 'T cells', which are part of the immune response to disease.

It was found during experimentation that tai chi practitioners produced more antibodies after exercising with the solo form. Athletes, on the other hand, appeared to have a lower antibody reading after running 1500 metres than they had before beginning the run. This could support the long held belief that tai chi assists in the body's ability to resist disease.

How to practise tai chi

The tai chi form requires that your posture be balanced and stable and your movements harmonious. You will observe that you have not over-exerted yourself and that your breathing is steady. With practice you should feel exhilarated and energetic.

The tai chi form should be fluid and continuous, even during position changes, giving the appearance of a slow, flowing river. Keep all of your movements round and smooth. This will give ease and strength to your posture, and your energy will be able to flow unimpeded. (There should be no dead steps throughout the exercise.)

Both the arms and legs should be co-ordinated. The movements should originate from the body and synchronise with the arms and legs.

Allow the breathing to be natural - do not try to control it.

Rules for practice

Use the conscious mind to guide the movements - 'The mind should lead the body'. This will develop deep concentration.

When practising the form, feel yourself making the movement slightly before you perform it. In this way you will be engaging the mind as well as the body. Without this 'leading' of the movements, you will not be practising tai chi correctly.

Do not allow your thoughts to scatter. Keep your thinking on the exercise at hand. Exclude all extraneous interference.

Check your posture:

1 is your breathing natural and centred in the lower abdomen?
2 is your head held up and are your shoulders relaxed?
3 are your spine and torso upright?
4 is your weight evenly distributed on two feet to begin the exercise?

Perform the tai chi solo exercise in a quiet and tranquil place. Noise will not allow the mind to be still and uninterrupted.

Concentrate only on the tai chi movements. Each technique should be performed as perfectly as possible, linking one with another, not allowing one technique to be any more important than those following or preceding.

Eventually the body will respond to the mind, performing the exercise more smoothly and accurately.

When your thinking is disturbed by anxiety or agitated in some way, do not practise. Allow your thinking to return to normal before exercising with tai chi.

Relaxation

When you are told to relax, this does not mean that your body should be limp: the spine should be straight and the head upright.

Generally, your posture should be 'correct' - not leaning to the left or right, forwards or backwards. Use only enough energy to perform the movement correctly, i.e. with the bare minimum of effort.

As you move through the exercises, feel as if your arms are floating.

Mind and body co-ordination

As the mind forms the idea of making the movement before the actual physical action, the tai chi student will be led into a whole body discipline. Having to mould these actions into the form, the mind and body will become united, opening up untold possibilities, spiritually and physically. If one part of the body moves, all parts move; no part is separated from the whole. This is the characteristic of Yang tai chi.

At the beginning, learn one step at a time. Memorise each posture, mentally and physically, before you move on to the next. When you have done this, join the movements together as a flowing whole.

Weight distribution and body movement

The shifting of the body weight and solidity of stances is very important when moving from one technique to another. The foot which has the weight upon it is said to be 'full', and the one which carries the least weight is said to be 'empty'. The tai chi form is in constant flux between empty and full steps. The transition from one to the other is very important in that if it is carried out correctly, it will create smoothness and continuity.

With this evenness of movement, your steps should be as light as a cat's. Be sure your stance is stable before turning left or right. Place your empty foot lightly, as if you are testing the ground. Slowly, move the weight on to the empty foot until it becomes full (i.e. most of the weight is on it). Thus your steps will be agile and your movements nimble.

Breathe and move from the tan tien

The centre of all movement and breathing in tai chi is the *tan tien* - a point two inches below the navel on the inside of the body. This is not only the centre of balance in human beings, but also in Oriental thinking the centre of *chi* (vital energy activity). There should be gentle concentration on this point while you are performing tai chi.

Breathing should be natural and calming. Do not try to slow it down - allow the breathing to do as it wishes- as you practise the form. The body will naturally gain a rhythm and depth from the tai chi movements. (*See also* pp. 150-1.)

Posture

A strong posture is of the upmost importance. The upright position allows the *chi* to circulate freely. If the posture is bent, twisted or in some way restricted, the energy will be blocked. It is helpful to imagine a hose-pipe that has a kink: the water will be either stopped completely or will come in spurts; when the kink is removed the water moves freely and with power.

We will begin at the top, with the head. If the head is held upright the body can be maintained in a stable upright position and the balance stabilised.

The head

Hold the head as if it were suspended from above. This mental imagery will allow the head to be supported with the least amount of muscular tension, because the body will react naturally to the mental image rather than trying to impose a rigid discipline if you 'try' to hold it upright.

Move your head in unison with the body. The head should not be allowed to move separately from the body.

Pull the chin in slightly and allow the jaw to relax. The facial muscles should be soft, without expression. Rest the tongue on the hard palate in the roof of the mouth.

Look in the direction in which your techniques are being directed. Be aware of your surroundings, but not overly so.

The shoulders and upper back

Allow your shoulders to hang in a relaxed fashion, but without bending your upper spine. This will facilitate breathing as well as relaxing the upper body.

The chest and abdomen

The chest and abdomen should be relaxed, which will cause the breathing to sink to the *tan tien*. With practice this will result in a pleasant warmth in the area; this warmth is the stirring of the *chi*.

The spine

It is vital that the spine is held erect because it is the central pillar of the body. Whatever the physical action - sitting or twisting - the spine plays a vital pivotal role.

For the body and the limbs to move in unison, it is essential that you have a straight spine. Again, the spine is as relaxed as possible, but you 'feel' it straight. Remember, what the mind *thinks* the body will *do*.

The lower back should also be straightened out. This is achieved by gently tucking the bottom under, which has the effect of taking the hollow out of the back. Do this gently! At first it will feel odd, but you will become accustomed to it. An added advantage of straightening out this area of the spine is that it strengthens that area, which will leave you less prone to injury.

Looking at the spine in its normal 'S' shape, most of the weight is taken in the lumbar region. It is in this area that most back trouble occurs. Flattening out this section results in a straightening of the spine; the pressure of the body's weight can be distributed equally among all of the vertebrae.

The legs

If you cannot stand you cannot walk, states an old martial arts saying. Pay special attention to the feet in the tai chi form - this is the root of bodily motion.

The chi is rooted in the feet,
Springs from the legs,
Guided by the waist,
Expressed in the hands.   (Tai chi poem)

Stabilise the feet and legs. Do not allow the knees to bend inwards. The only movement at the knees should be as nature intended - forwards and backwards, not side to side. When moving forwards the heel should touch first; when moving backwards the toes should land first. Neglecting your footwork will ruin the flow of the form totally.

The arms

Let the elbows hang down, states a tai chi maxim. By doing so, the shoulders will relax and sink down. With your shoulders down, the elbows will relax naturally in turn.

Leave a gap of one fist width at the armpits (approximately three inches). Test this by placing the fist under the armpit and allow the arm to rest against the fist. Closing this point, so that the arm is allowed to touch the body, would prevent the *chi* from circulating freely.

Never straighten the elbows completely when pushing out - leave a small bend in them.

Hold the wrists naturally - do not allow them to drop.

Your shoulder joints should be relaxed - allow the body to do the work.

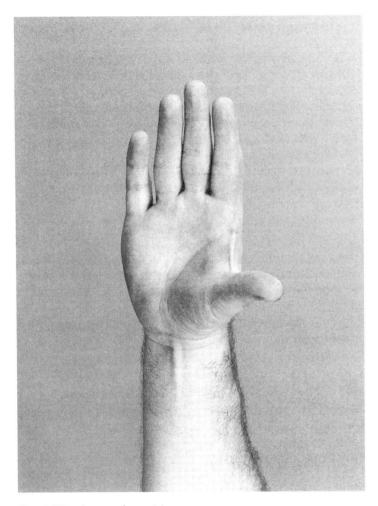

Fig. 2 Tiger's mouth position

The hand should be held in the 'tiger's mouth' position (fig. 2). Stretch the hand by pulling back the thumbs and extending the fingers. A flap of skin will appear between the thumb and the index finger which resembles the mouth of a tiger, hence the name. This hand position hollows out the palm and is sometimes called the 'tile palm'.

Perseverance

Practise every day, either in the morning or evening. Try not to miss out days because this will hamper your progress. Tai chi is meant to be *used,* not simply learned. The longer you practise tai chi correctly, the more perfect it will become, and the greater the benefits.

Attend a good tai chi class if possible: the benefit of good first-hand tuition can be significant.

If you have friends you can practise with, so much the better. Company during training can see you through the 'bad' days. Once the form is mastered and the benefits become apparent, you will need no outside encouragement. Tai chi will become an essential part of your day, just like washing or cleaning your teeth.

Select a quiet, clean place to exercise, preferably in the open air. The best places are under trees, where the air is pure. Do not train in the wind or in the damp.

Practising inside is quite acceptable, especially during bad weather. Make certain that the room is well ventilated and warm. Protect yourself from drafts.

Speed

We are using the classical Yang tai chi slow form. When practising, move as if you were walking through water or watching a slow motion replay. 'Slow', 'smooth' and 'constant' should be your watchwords. Do not alter the tempo when you are changing position.

The Yang style long form takes 12 to 15 minutes to complete, although 14 minutes is the optimum time.

Movement in the form

Always keep the knees bent and move smoothly forwards or backwards. Do not look down, just straight ahead. Keep the same height while practising - straightening the knees will make you bob up and down, which will break the flow and make your form appear clumsy.

Warm-up

A warm-up routine is essential to any exercise regime, whether it be gentle or strenuous. Tight muscles and stiff joints are not conducive to the flowing movements of tai chi, which require the body to be at ease. A gentle warm-up will leave you ready for the solo form, both mentally and physically. Loosenedup joints will function that much better, and warm and flexible muscles will respond in the way you would wish. Remember that tai chi is body and mind in total harmony. When the body is moving well the mind can be at ease. It is the flow and rhythm of movement which soothes the nervous system and calms the mind. With the calming of the mind, signals are sent throughout the body which encourage deep relaxation. A tenet of traditional Oriental medicine is: *The mind affects the body, and the body affects the mind* - the two are inseparable.

In our warm-up we will stretch the tendons and muscles gently, and loosen the joints and articulations. The internal organs benefit indirectly by receiving a soft massage from the twisting movements.

Although this warm-up is very gentle, if you have any doubts about your ability to perform any actions in this book, please consult a doctor prior to commencement.

Points to remember
1 Perform the exercises **slowly** and **smoothly**.
2 Go only as far as you feel comfortable. If you are unused to exercise, begin easily and gradually increase as and when you feel fit.

Fig. 3 Clasp your hands together in front of you. Spread your feet one shoulder width wide, weight evenly distributed.

Fig. 4 Slowly swing your hands to the left and to the right as far as they will go naturally. Do not push the rotation beyond its current limit. Perform five swings to the left and five to the right. When you have completed your ten rotations, finish with your hands still clasped in front of you.

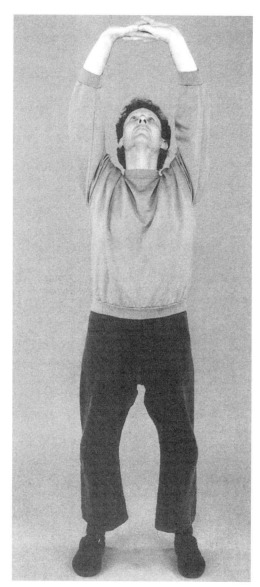

Fig. 5 From your previous position, bend forwards and downwards and try to touch the floor in front of you with the palms. It doesn't matter whether you do touch the floor or not - simply the act of stretching is the most important thing. Go only as far as you can without putting undue stress on your back.

Fig. 6 From your previous position, bend your knees slightly and swing your arms up over your head and stretch. Repeat figs 5 and 6 five times in a flowing, smooth action.

Fig. 7 Place your left hand on your left hip, with the elbow bent. Extend your right arm straight up, to rest against your right ear.

Fig. 8 Stretch as far as comfortable towards your left side, taking the pressure of the bend on your bent left elbow. Your back should feel only the stretch, not your body weight. You will feel the muscles on your right side stretch in this movement. Return to the upright position and repeat five times, slowly and smoothly. Change hands so that your right hand is placed against your right hip, with your right elbow flexed and your left arm straight up. Repeat the stretch to the right side five times as before.

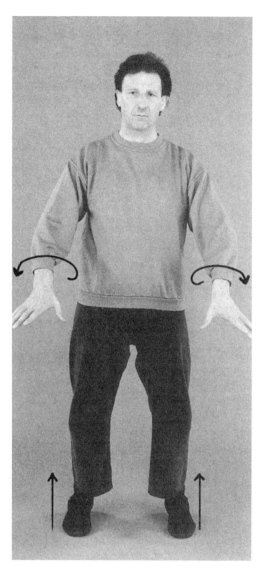

Fig. 9 Stand up on your toes with both of your hands extended forwards and the elbows bent. Rotate your hands outwards in a circle, five times for both hands. When you have completed this, rotate the hands inwards five times. As you are turning your hands, try to feel the stretch in your wrists as much as possible. This exercise will help to prevent stiffness in the wrists.

Fig. 10 Place all of your weight on to your left leg and extend both hands in front of you, with the elbows bent. Keeping your knee straight, lift your right leg approximately 12 inches (30 cm) from the ground. Rotate your right ankle, five times to the right and five times to the left. Place your right leg down and repeat the same exercise with the left ankle.

Fig. 11 On completion of the previous exercise, place both of your hands together as if in prayer. Lift your left leg, placing it just above your right knee, and balance in this position for 15 seconds. When you have completed the exercise, change legs and repeat for the other leg.

Fig. 12 Extend both of your hands in front of you, with the palms facing down. Swing your right leg up as high as you can without strain and attempt to touch the palm of your right hand. As your right foot touches the ground, swing your left leg up in the same fashion. Repeat five times for each leg. Raise only as high as you feel is comfortable; increase the height as you become more able.

Fig. 13 Extend your hands to the sides, with your palms facing down. Swing your right leg up and try to touch the right palm with the toes of your right foot. As your right foot touches the ground, swing your left foot up and try to touch your left palm. Repeat five times for each foot. If you cannot touch the palms, don't worry - it is the act of raising the leg as high as you can which will stretch the tendons.

Figs 14 and 15 Extend your feet two shoulder widths apart, parallel to each other. Bend your knees and sink your weight equally on to both feet. Place your hands on top of your pelvis and lean forwards. Swing your body to the left, keeping your weight evenly placed on both feet. Continue the rotation backwards and to the right until you end up where you started. From this position, swing your body to the right in exactly the same fashion, until you end up in the bent forward position as before. Repeat the exercise to the left and to the right, five times in each direction. Take this exercise slowly, especially during the early stages of your training.

Stances

Before we can proceed on to the tai chi solo form, a basic knowledge of the stances used in Yang tai chi is essential. Without the skilful application of the correct stances, your tai chi will look and feel clumsy. The smooth interaction of the upper and lower body is critical for the circulation of *chi* and the maintenance of continuity. The self-defence applications would lose much of their effectiveness without the generation of total body co-ordination to maximise power.

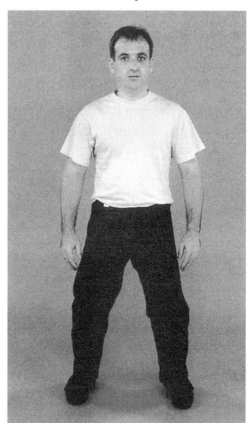

Natural stance

Fig. 16 Place your weight evenly on both feet, at a distance of one shoulder width, with the feet parallel. Your knees should be bent such that they just obscure your toes when looking down.

Forward stance

Fig. 17 80% of your weight should be on your front foot, with your knee bent enough to just obscure your toes from view. The width of the stance should be one shoulder width wide and two of your foot lengths from the heel of your front foot to the toe of your back foot. Your back foot should be at an angle of 45°, with the knee directly in line with the toes when you look down.

Back stance

Fig. 18 The back stance is approximately half a shoulder width wide, with 60% of your weight on your back leg and 40% on your front leg. The back foot is at an angle of 45° and your front foot points directly forwards. The length of your stance is approximately half that of the forward stance.

Toe up stance

Fig. 19 70% of your weight should be on your back foot, with your foot at a 45° angle. Your front foot points directly forwards with your foot raised up and resting on the heel. The length of your stance is fractionally shorter than the back stance, at approximately three-quarters of your foot length.

Cat stance

Fig. 20 80% of your weight rests on your back foot, with your foot at a 45° angle. Your front foot should have its heel raised, resting on the toes and pointing directly forwards. The length and width of the stance is the same as the toe up stance.

Snake creeps down stance

Fig. 21 Approximately 90% of your weight rests on your back foot, with the foot pointing backwards. Your front knee points directly forwards and is slightly bent. This stance tends to be deeper than the others, but remember to stand only as low as feels comfortable.

Snake stance

Fig. 22 80% of your weight rests on your back foot, with your foot at a 45° angle. Your front foot should be turned in as far as it can comfortably go. The leg is straight. Remember: if you have not exercised for some time, stand in a stance which feels comfortable and does not exert excessive strain. With consistent practice, you will find that taking up the stance becomes easier.

The tai chi solo form

Directions

For ease of understanding, we will use the points of the compass for the directions of the form. In fig. 23 you will be facing **north**, on your right will be **east**, to your left **west** and behind you **south**. Unless the text states specifically that you perform movements at the same time, carry them out one after another.

Section one

Move 1

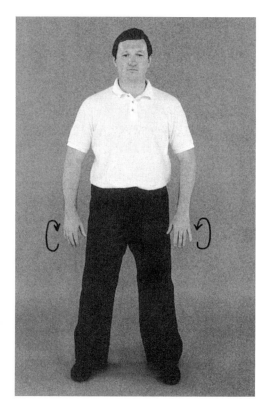

Fig. 23 (*Beginning*) Take up a natural stance, with your feet one shoulder width apart and the weight evenly distributed. Your hands hang naturally by your sides with the elbows held out a fraction. You are facing north.

Move 2

Fig. 24 (*Lift hands*) Move your hands forwards and backwards in a small circle, finishing at your hips. Immediately lift your hands up in front of you to shoulder height, with the hands hanging down. This movement should feel as if the wrists are being lifted for you - little effort should be exhibited on your part.

Move 4

Move 3

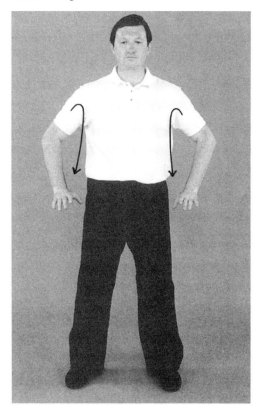

Fig. 25 As your hands reach the height of your shoulders, pull your wrists towards you. At approximately six inches (15 cm) from your shoulders, continue the motion of your hands downwards, ending as they began, in line with your hips.

Fig. 26 Turn your waist to the right, allowing your hands to circle round with the motion of your body. At this point your left hand should be in line with your right leg, and your right hand should be behind your right hip. You are facing north-east.

Move 5

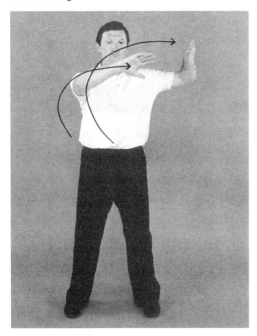

Move 6

Fig. 27 *(Grasp tail)* Without stopping the motion, circle your hands upwards and to the left. Your right palm is now pointing to the north. Your left palm is facing west and your fingers point north.

Fig. 28 ABOVE RIGHT Bend your knees and shift most of your weight on to your left foot. As you do so, turn your right palm down and press your left hand down by the side of your left hip.

Move 7

Fig. 29 Turn your right foot out to the north-east. Rotate your body to the right as you shift your weight on to your right foot. In this position your left hand is in line with your right hip and your right hand is to the right of your face. You are facing north-east.

Move 8

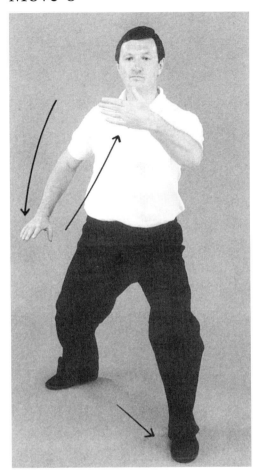

Fig. 30 *(Ward off slantingly upward/grasp tail)* Transfer all of your weight on to your right foot. Move your left foot directly forwards to the north. Sweep your left hand to the north, moving into a forward stance. As your left hand is moving forwards your right hand should be travelling down near to your right hip. in all movements of the form, when your hand is placed by your hip, it is at a distance of one palm width. You are facing north.

Move 9

Fig. 31 Turn your left palm down as you move your right hand to the north to finish directly under your left palm, with 18 inches (45 cm) separating them. Both hands are in line with your right leg. Shift all of your weight on to your left foot and move your right foot half a step towards the north. Raise your hands with the palms facing each other. Both hands are in line with your left shoulder. This is the preparation for *double hand grasp tail* (move 10). To the east.

Move 10

Fig. 32 *(Double hand grasp tail)* Transfer your weight on to your right foot and slowly move your hands forwards to the east. Your left hand is in line with your right elbow crease, and it should feel as if you are holding an invisible ball. To the east.

Move 11

Fig. 33 *(Pull back)* Turn your left palm up and your right palm down as you shift your weight into a back stance. As you move into the back stance, pull your hands back towards your hip. The left hand is pointing to the east and the right hand to the north and they are approximately 15 inches (40 cm) apart. To the east.

Move 12

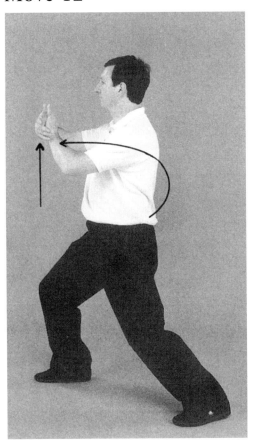

Fig. 34 *(Press)* Lift both of your hands up in line with your left shoulder. Move your left hand forwards to touch your right wrist and transfer your weight into a right forward stance to the east. Press both of your hands forwards as you move into the forward stance. Your hands are now in line with your chest. To the east.

Move 13

Fig. 35 Shift your weight back on to your left leg, while turning your palms down and pulling them back towards your chest. To the east.

Move 14

Fig. 36 *(Push)* Move your hands down to chest level and shift into a forward stance, moving both of your palms forwards to the east. Your hands should be one shoulder width apart. To the east.

Move 15

Fig. 37 *(Ward off to the left)* As you shift your weight into a left snake stance, sweep both of your hands to the northwest. Your hands are at the level of your chin, with your left palm facing northwest and your right fingers in line with your left elbow crease. To the northwest.

Move 16

Fig. 38 *(Ward off to the right)* Transfer your weight into a right snake stance as you sweep your hands to the south-east. This should be a mirror image of the previous movement. To the south-east.

Move 17

Fig. 39 Turn your right palm up and join your fingers together. Circle your right hand down as you turn your left palm up. Lift your left heel off of the ground. With all of your weight on your right foot, rotate your body to the left, pivoting on the ball of your left foot. This is the preparation to *single whip* (move 18). To the north-west.

Move 18

Move 19

Fig. 40 *(Single whip)* Move your left leg one step across to the south. Shift your weight into a left forward stance as you move your left palm to the west. To the west.

Fig. 41 *(Raise hands)* Pivot on your left heel as you turn your left foot north-west and move your left hand across to the north. Transfer your weight on to your left foot and move your right leg across half a step, with your right hand moving directly in front of the body. Your left hand is in line with the inside of your right elbow, and both hands point to the north. You are in a toe up stance. To the north.

Move 20

Move 21

Move 22

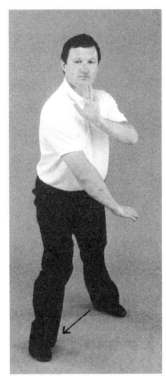

Fig. 42 *(Pull back)* Perform *pull back* as before (move 11), except your right toes should still be raised. To the north.

Fig. 43 Circle your left hand out to the left and then across in front of your face. This is the preparation for *shoulder stroke* (move 22). To the north.

Fig. 44 *(Shoulder stroke)* Move your right foot half a step diagonally to the right, shifting into a forward stance and turning the right shoulder forwards. Your body should be leaning forwards slightly to the north.

Move 23

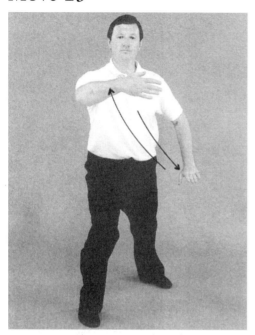

Move 24

Fig. 45 *(Ward off slantingly upward)*
Sweep your left hand down and back near your left hip, as you move your right hand out towards the north.

Fig. 46 ABOVE RIGHT *(Crane spreads wings)*
Shift your weight on to your right foot and turn your body to the left, as
your left foot moves into a cat stance. As you move your left foot, sweep your left hand down near to your left hip and your right hand up near your right temple. You are now facing west.

Move 25

Fig. 47 Circle your right hand across your body, past your left shoulder and down back near your right hip. Circle your left hand across to the centre of the body, with your fingers pointing up. These movements should flow from one to the other.

Move 26

Fig. 48 *(Brush knee right)* Move your left palm down in line with your chest as you continue to circle your right hand back and up near to your right ear. Move your left foot out one step diagonally to the west and as you shift your weight into a forward stance, move your right palm to the west and pull your left palm near to your left hip. To the west.

Move 27

Fig. 49 *(Raise hands play the lute)* Shift your weight on to your left foot and raise your right heel 12 inches (30 cm) from the ground. Place your right foot down and lift up your left hand. As you move into a toe up stance, your right hand turns to the south and drops to chest level. This movement is almost the same as *raise hands* (move 19), except the front hand moves *up* rather than across. To the west.

Move 28

Fig. 50 *(Brush knee right)* Circle your right hand back and repeat *brush knee* with your right palm.

Move 29

Fig. 51 *(Hold the ball to the left)* Pivoting on your left heel, turn your left foot south-west. Turn your body to the southwest, placing your left hand above your left knee - palm up - and your right hand above it - palm down - in line with your left shoulder. 80% of your weight is on your left leg. To the south-west.

Move 30

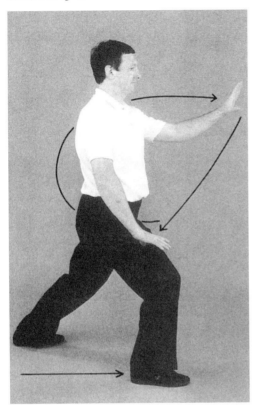

Fig. 52 *(Brush knee left)* Step forwards with your right foot towards the west. Circle your left hand back towards the east and then forwards to the west, shifting into a right forward stance. You have now performed *brush knee* to the left. To the west.

Move 31

Fig. 53 *(Hold the ball to the right)* Pivot on your right heel as you turn your right foot to the north-west. At the same time place your right hand above the right knee - palm up - as your left hand positions itself - palm down - in line with your right shoulder and directly above your right hand. To the north-west.

Move 32

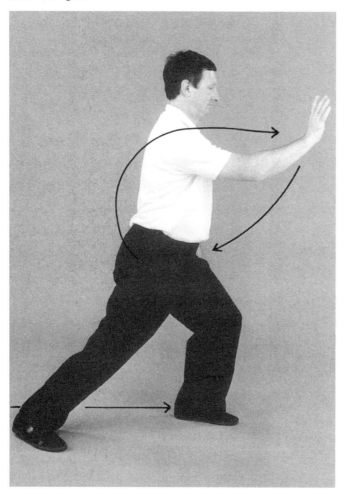

Move 33
Repeat move 27.

Move 34
Repeat move 28.

Fig. 54 *(Brush knee right)* Move your left foot forwards one step towards the west and repeat *brush knee right,* as before. To the west.

Move 35

Move 36

Move 37

Fig. 55 *(Parry down and hit with fist)* Turn your left foot to the south-west as you pivot on your left heel. As you turn your left foot, turn your right palm over, lightly closing it into a fist near your left hip. At the same time, close your right hand into a fist and point it down. To the southwest.

Fig. 56 ABOVE RIGHT Step forwards with your right foot towards the west. As you do so, circle your right fist to the west and open your left hand, circling it up near to your left ear. You are in a back stance.

Fig. 57 Shift your weight into a right forward stance and move your left palm towards the west, while pulling your right fist to the right hip.

Move 38

Move 39

Fig. 58 *(Parry and punch)* Turn your right foot out to the north-west and take one step forwards with your left foot, towards the west. As you move forwards, turn your right palm in, shift your weight into a left forward stance and punch forwards with your right fist while pulling back your left palm near the right elbow crease.

Fig. 59 ABOVE RIGHT Slip your left hand behind your right elbow.

Move 40

Fig. 60 Open your right hand and slide your left hand towards the west. Continue the movement by shifting your weight back on to your right leg and circling both of your hands out and back towards your chest.

Move 41

Fig. 61 *(Close the door)* Shift your weight into a left forward stance as you push both palms forwards to the west. Your hands are one shoulder width apart.

Move 42

Fig. 62 Shift your weight on to a right snake stance as you turn your body to the north and move your hands apart slightly wider than your shoulders.

Move 43

Fig. 63 *(Cross hands)* Shift your weight on to your left foot and move your right foot back parallel to your left foot. Move your weight into a natural stance and circle both of your hands down and then up, crossing at your wrists. Your hands are at the level of your throat. You are facing north.

For teaching purposes this is the end of section one. But once you have learned this section, you should carry on into the next as if it were one, with *no* obvious break in the movements.

Section two   Move 44

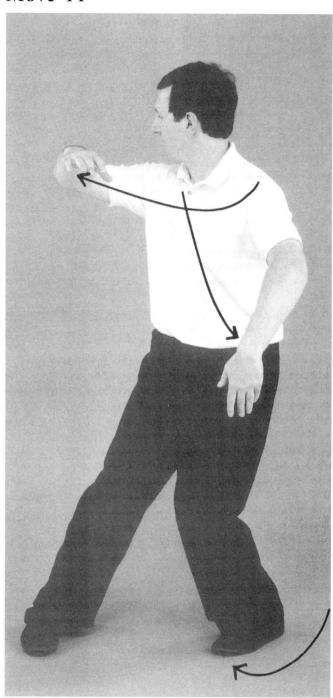

Fig. 64 Circle your left hand down in line with your left hip as you pivot on your left heel and turn your left foot in as far as possible. This is the preparation for *carry tiger to the mountain* (move 45).

Move 45

Fig. 65 *(Carry tiger to the mountain)* Move your right foot one step towards the south-east. As you do so, raise your left hand up in line with your left ear. Shift your weight into a right forward stance, pushing your left palm towards the south-east and pulling your right hand back by your hip. This movement is similar to *brush knee.*

Move 46

Fig. 66 Turn your left hand over - palm up - as you circle your right hand towards the south-east.

Move 47

Repeat move 11.
To the south-east.

Move 48

Repeat move 12.
To the south-east.

Move 49

Repeat move 13.
To the south-east.

Move 50

Repeat move 14.
To the south-east.

Move 51

Turn to the north-west.
Repeat move 15.

Move 52

Turn to the south-east.
Repeat move 16.

Move 53

Fig. 67 *(Holding up the sky)* Place your weight on to your right foot and move your left foot one step to the north-west. As you turn your body to the left, swing both of your hands down and up to the north-west and move into a forward stance.

Move 54

Fig. 68 With your weight on your left foot, sweep your right foot to the north-east, ending in a snake stance. You are facing north-west.

Move 55

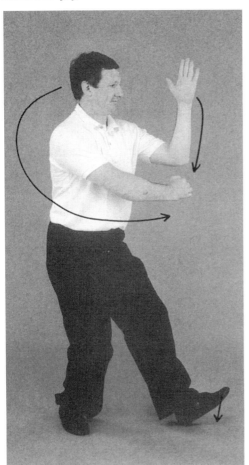

Fig. 69 *(Fist under the elbow)* Shift your weight on to your right foot and move your left foot half a step to the right, in a toe up stance. Close your right hand into a fist, circling it down and to the west, under your left elbow. You face west.

Move 56

Fig. 70 Turn your left palm up and circle your right hand down and back to the east, at shoulder height. Both of your palms face upwards.

Move 57

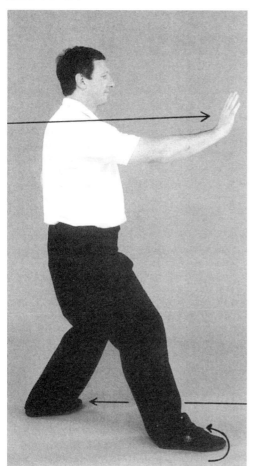

Fig. 71 *(Repulse monkey right)* Take your left foot back one step to the east. As you sit into a left back stance, push your right palm to the west and pull your left palm to your left hip - palm up.

Move 58

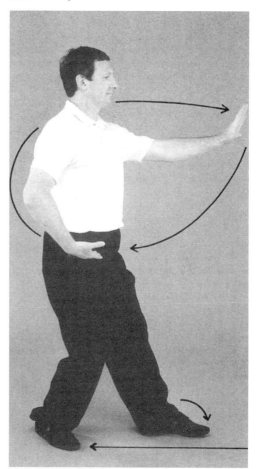

Fig. 72 *(Repulse monkey left)* Circle your left hand back to the east and up to shoulder height. Step back with your right foot to the east and as you move into a back stance, push to the west with your left palm and pull your right (upturned) palm to the right hip.

Move 59

Fig. 73 *(Repulse monkey right)* Turn your left palm up as you circle your right hand back and up as before. Step back with your left foot and repeat move 57.

Move 60

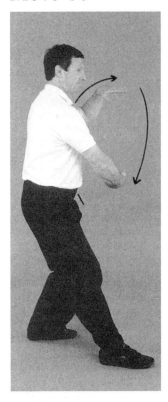

Fig. 74 *(Hold the ball)* Rotate your right palm to the left and your left palm to the right, so that both palms face each other, as if you are holding a large ball. Still with this notion of the ball in mind, circle your right hand down in front of your left hip and at the same time circle your left hand up in line with your left shoulder. Both palms face each other: it is as if you have rotated the large imaginary ball over and above your left knee.

Move 61

Fig. 75 *(Part the wild horse's mane)* Place your weight on to your left foot and sweep your right foot over to the north-east. As you shift your weight into a right forward stance, sweep your right hand across to the north-east in a scything motion. As your right hand sweeps out, pull your left hand down by your left hip. You face north-east.

Move 62

Fig. 76 *(Raise hands)* Shift your weight back on to your left foot and move your right foot across to the left in a toe up stance. As you move your right foot across, lift your left hand forwards and upwards in line with your chest and move your right hand across in front of your left hand. This is a repetition of move 19. You are facing north.

Move 63

Repeat move 20.
Facing north.

Move 64

Repeat move 21.
Facing north.

Move 65

Repeat move 22.
Facing north.

Move 66

Repeat move 23.
Facing north.

Move 67

Repeat move 24.
Facing west.

Move 68

Repeat move 25.
Facing north.

Move 69

Repeat move 26.

Move 70

Fig. 77 Shift your weight on to your left foot and lift your right heel approximately 12 inches (30 cm) from the ground. Place your right foot down and shift your weight on to the right foot. As you shift your weight back, lift up your left toes and point your right fingers down. You are in a toe up stance.

Move 71

Fig. 78 *(Needle at sea bottom)* Move your left toes back slightly into a cat stance. Bend forwards from your hips and extend your right fingers towards the ground. To the west.

Move 72

Fig. 79 *(Fan through the back)* Straighten your body upright and move your hands up to chest level. Both of your palms point towards the west, with your right hand slightly higher than your left. Shift your left foot half a step diagonally to the west. As you move into a left forward stance, press your left palm to the west and pull your right hand up in line with your temple, palm facing out.

Move 73

Fig. 80 *(Yin Yang hand)* **Next two moves** Close your right hand into a fist and shift your weight into a right snake stance as you turn your body and left foot to the north and move your left (open) hand in front of your right fist. Both your right fist and your left palm face the north.

Move 74

Fig. 81 Shift your weight into a left snake stance and move your hands in line with your left shoulder.

Move 75

Move 76

Fig. 82 *(Parry down and hit with fist)* Move your right foot across one step to the south and move your fist back to the east. You are in a right back stance.

Fig. 83 ABOVE RIGHT Move into a right forward stance. Press your left palm towards the east as you pull your right fist back to your right hip.

Move 77

Fig. 84 Turn your body to the right and pull your left palm back near to your right hip. When your left palm reaches your right hip, move your right fist directly to the east, palm facing up. This is called a 'driving punch' or 'uppercut'.

Move 78

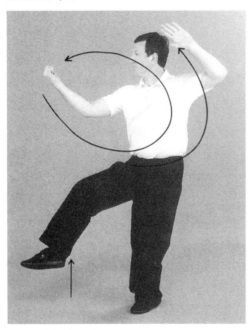

Move 79

Fig. 85 *(Hit down and parry)* Shift your weight on to your left foot and at the same time turn your right hand down and your left palm up. Sweep your hands back and up, lifting your right foot to knee height with your toes pointing to the south-east.

Move 80

Fig. 86 ABOVE RIGHT Place your right foot down with 80% of your weight upon it and move your fist back to the east. Your left hand is near to your left ear.

Fig. 87 Move your palm towards the east and move your right fist to your right hip.

Move 81

Fig. 88 *(Parry and punch)* Step forwards with your left foot and repeat move 38. To the east.

Move 82

Fig. 89 Circle your left hand behind your right elbow.

Move 83

Fig. 90 *(Separate hands obliquely)*
Simultaneously turn your body and your left foot to the north-east, pivoting on your left heel as you sweep your upturned left palm in the same direction and move your right palm down by your right hip.

Move 84

Fig. 91 Take a step towards the east with your right foot, at the same time circling your right hand towards the north. As you make the movement, move your left hand in line with your left shoulder, with your left palm facing the east. Your right palm faces west and it feels as if you are holding a ball. You are in a back stance.

Move 85

Repeat move 10.
To the east.

Move 86

Repeat move 11.
To the east.

Move 87

Repeat move 12.
To the east.

Move 88

Repeat move 13.
To the east.

Move 89

Repeat move 14.
To the east.

Move 90

Repeat move 15.
To the north-west.

Move 91

Repeat move 16.
To the south-east.

Move 92

Repeat move 17.
To the north-west.

Move 93

Repeat move 18.
To the west.

Move 94

Fig. 92 With your weight on your left heel, turn your left toes and left palm to the north, as your right palm flattens down.

Move 95

Fig. 93 Shift all of your weight on to your left foot, press your left palm down and circle your right hand - palm up - in line with your left elbow. At the same time, move your right foot in half a step to the west. You face north.

Move 96

Fig. 94 *(Wave hands like clouds 1)* Shift 80% of your weight on to your right foot and, at the same time, circle your right hand past your face to the east and your left hand down and to the east. Your right palm is facing your right shoulder and your left hand is in line with your right hip. Point your left fingers to the north.

Move 97

Fig. 95 As soon as your hands pass over your right knee, move your left foot half a step to the west.

Move 98

Fig. 96 Shift 80% of your weight on to your left foot. Circle your left hand up and to the left, and your right hand down in line with your left hip. At the same time move your right foot in half a step to the west. Your left palm is facing your left shoulder and the heel of your right palm is in line with your left hip.

Move 99

(Wave hands like clouds 2)
Repeat move 96.

Move 100

Repeat move 97.

Move 101

Repeat move 98.

Move 102

(Wave hands like clouds 3)
Repeat move 96.

Move 103

Repeat move 97.

Move 104

Repeat move 98.

Move 105

Fig. 97 *(Looking in the mirror)* Move your weight on to your right foot, circling your right hand up near your right shoulder and your left hand down and up inside your right hand. Both of your palms are facing in towards you, with the palm of your right hand facing the back of your left hand. Your left fingers are in line with your right elbow crease.

Move 106

Repeat move 18. To the west.

Move 107

Fig. 98 Shift your weight into a left toe up stance and turn both of your palms up.

Move 108

Fig. 99 *(Pat the high horse)* Draw your left foot back into a cat stance. Move your right hand to the west and pull your left hand back to your left hip at the same time. The movement with your right hand is called a 'cut' and the striking surface is the edge of your hand. When performing this movement, your fingers should skim close to your ear as it travels past.

Move 109

Fig. 100 *(Hold the ball)* Turn your body to the north-west and move your right hand in line with your right shoulder and your left hand near to your right hip. Your right palm is directly above your left palm. You are facing north-west.

Move 110

Fig. 101 Lift your left hand up so that it passes on the outside of your right hand. Move your left foot out to the southwest. As you shift into a left forward stance, pull your left palm near to your left temple and 'cut' to the north-west with your right hand.

Move 111

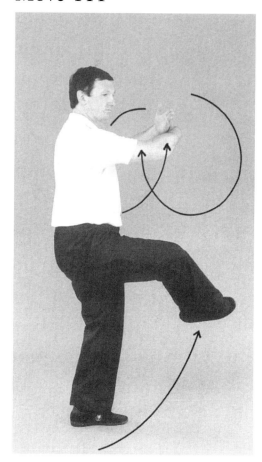

Fig. 102 Transfer your weight on to your left foot and lift your right foot up as you circle your right hand up to the south-west. Your right hand now forms an 'X' with your left. Your right foot should be flexed in, so that a hollow appears at the inner side of the ankle. Position your right foot approximately ten inches (25 cm) from your left knee.

Move 112

Fig. 103 *(Lotus kick)* Continue to circle your hands out to the sides. Your left hand points to the south-east and the right hand points to the north-west. As you complete this movement, sweep your right foot to the north-west.

Move 113

Fig. 104 Pull your right foot in and place it down into a forward stance with your right foot pointing to the north-west. Your hands hold the positions from the kick. Your body is facing south-west.

Move 114

Fig. 105 Move your left hand 12 inches (30 cm) towards the north-west. Then sweep your right hand down towards the south-east and up towards the north-west, passing the left hand on the outside. As your right hand passes your left, cut to the south-west with your left hand. This is the same action as in move 110, but now on the left side.

Move 115

Fig. 106 Circle your left hand down and up to the north-west so that the hands form an 'X' as you lift the left foot.

Move 116

Fig. 107 *(Lotus kick)* Sweep the top of the left foot to the south-west. This is the left-sided version of move 112.

Move 117

Fig. 108 Pull your left foot in and place it behind your right foot, with your left heel facing east. Pivot to the east on the ball of your left foot and the right heel.

Move 118

Fig. 109 *(Lift knee and kick with heel)*
Make complete circles outwards with both of your hands and lift your left knee at the same time, pointing to the east. once your hands have completed the circles, kick your left foot to the east.

Move 119

Fig. 110 *(Brush knee right)* Pull your kick back and place your left foot down into a forward stance. As you do so, move your left hand down to your left hip and push towards the east with your right palm (as in move 28).

Move 120

Repeat move 29. To the north-east.

Move 121

Fig. 111 Repeat move 30. To the east.

Move 122

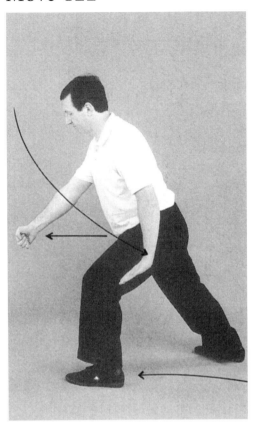

Fig. 112 *(Step up and hit down)* Close your right hand into a fist and touch it on the right thigh. At the same time turn your right foot out to the south-east. Step forwards with your left foot to the east and as you move into a left forward stance, sweep your left hand down to your left hip and move your right fist up to the east. You should lean your body slightly forwards as you move your right fist up.

Move 123

Move 124

Fig. 113 Repeat move 73. Facing south.

Fig. 114 ABOVE RIGHT Repeat move 74. Facing south.

Move 125

Fig. 115 Repeat move 75. To the west.

Move 126

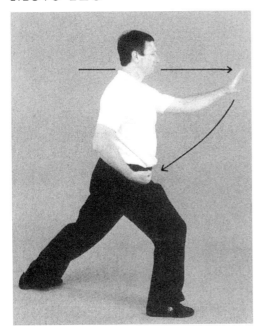

Move 127

Fig. 116 Repeat move 76. To the west.

Fig. 117 ABOVE RIGHT Repeat move 77.

Move 128

Fig. 118 Repeat move 78. To the west.

Move 129

Move 130

Fig. 119 Repeat move 79. To the west.

Fig. 120 ABOVE RIGHT Repeat move 80. To the west.

Move 131

Fig. 121 Repeat move 81. To the west.

Move 132

Repeat move 82.
To the west.

Move 133

Fig. 122 Repeat move 83. To the south-west.

Move 134

Fig. 123 *(Lift knee and kick with heel)*
Circle your right hand up to make an 'X' with your left hand and draw your foot near to your left leg. Move your hands out to the sides as before and kick to the north-west. This kick is performed in the same way as in move 118.

Move 135

Move 136

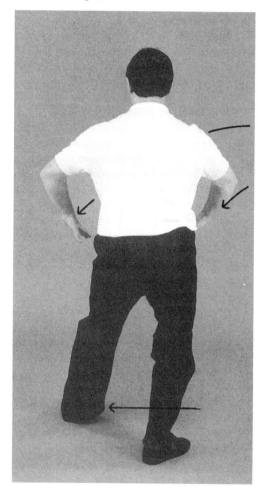

Fig. 124 *(Straight ward off)* Pull your right foot in and move it to the north-west. As you shift your weight into a right forward stance, press both of your palms to the north-west. This is the same hands position as in *ward off* to the right - the difference is that you are not in a snake stance.

Fig. 125 Shift all of your weight on to your right foot and move your left foot one step to the south-east. Turn your body to the south-east and allow your hands to turn with you and move down in front of you. Your hands are two feet (60 cm) in front of you and in line with their respective hips.

Move 137

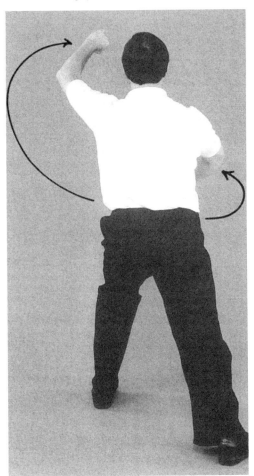

Fig. 126 *(Embrace tiger left)* Close both of your hands into fists and circle your hands out and in as you move into a left forward stance. Your left fist is in line with your left temple and your right fist is in line with your right ribs, both hands approximately 15 inches (40 cm) from your body.

Move 138

Fig. 127 Shift all of your weight on to your left foot and move your right foot one step across to the north-west. Open your hands and move them with the motion of your body, as in move 136.

Move 139

Move 140

Fig. 128 *(Embrace tiger right)* Close your hands into fists and move into a right forward stance, circling your hands out and in. Your right hand is in line with your right temple and your left hand is in line with your left lower ribs.

Fig. 129 ABOVE RIGHT Raise your left fist up in line with your right fist.

Move 141

Fig. 130 Transfer your weight on to your right foot and shift your left foot one step across to the east. Pivot on your right heel and shift your weight into a left forward stance, holding your hands in place. You are facing south. When you are moving into the forward stance and pivoting on your right heel, your right foot should also be turning to the left, thus completing a correct forward stance with the foot at a 45° angle.

Move 142

Fig. 131 *(Lift knee and kick with heel)*
Make complete circles with both hands
and kick with the heel to the west.

Move 143

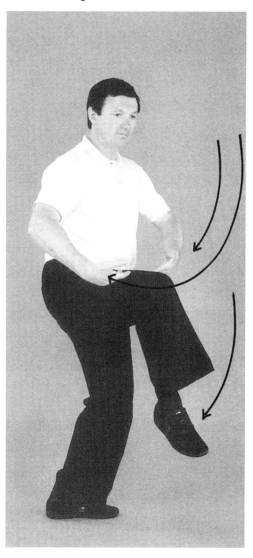

Fig. 132 Keeping your left foot still, turn
your body to the north-west and flick the
backs of your fingers downwards against
your right thigh.

Move 144

Fig. 133 *(Fists punch ears)* Place your right foot down in a right forward stance and circle both of your fists out and then in at the height of your temples. Your fists should be approximately 15 inches (40 cm) in front of you. You are now facing between north-west and north.

Fig. 134 *(Lift knee and kick with heel)* ABOVE RIGHT Turn your right foot to face the north by pivoting on your right heel and shifting all of your weight on to your right foot. Make complete circles with both of your hands. Lift your left knee and kick to the west.

Move 145

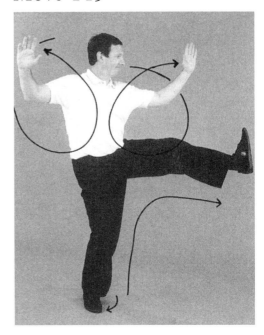

Move 146

Fig. 135 Pull your left foot back and take a large step to the east with this foot.

Move 147

Fig. 136 *(Lift knee and kick with heel)*
Turn your body 180° to the right. Your
hands are still out and you are facing west.
Circle your hands up and out, lift your
right knee and kick with your heel to the
west, as before.

Move 148

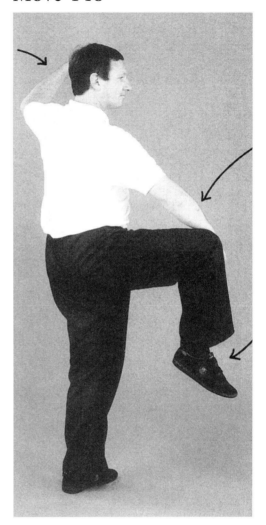

Fig. 137 Move your right leg back in and
let your right forearm rest on your raised
right thigh with your wrist hanging
loosely. Your left hand should be held up
and, again, your wrist should be hanging
loose.

Move 149

Repeat move 37, to the west, except that in this move the right palm is open and facing down, in a similar fashion to *brush knee*.

Move 150

Repeat move 38.
To the west.

Move 151

Repeat move 39.
To the west.

Move 152

Repeat move 40.
To the west.

Move 153

Repeat move 41.
To the west.

Move 154

Repeat move 42.

Move 155

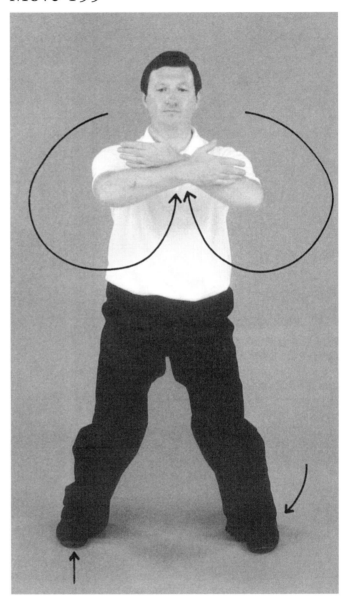

Fig. 138 *(Cross hands)* Repeat move 43.

This is the end of the second section. As before, once this is learned you should join the second and third sections together.

Section three

Move 156
Repeat move 44. To the south-east.

Move 157
Repeat move 45. To the south-east.

Move 158
Repeat move 46. To the south-east.

Move 159
Repeat move 47. To the south-east.

Move 160
Repeat move 48. To the south-east.

Move 161
Repeat move 49. To the south-east.

Move 162
Repeat move 50. To the south-east.

Move 163

Move 164

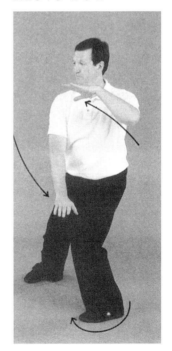

Fig. 139 *(Single whip)* ABOVE RIGHT Hook your right fingers together, turn your right palm up and your right foot in, pivoting on your right heel. Shift your weight on to your right foot and move your left foot one step over to the west. Perform *single whip* to the north-west. Do not forget to turn your right foot in as you move into the forward stance.

Fig. 140 Pivoting on your left heel, turn your left foot to the east. As you do so, move your left hand in line with your left shoulder, palm down and above your left knee. Open your right hand with your palm down and move it directly under your left palm and in line with your left hip.

Move 165

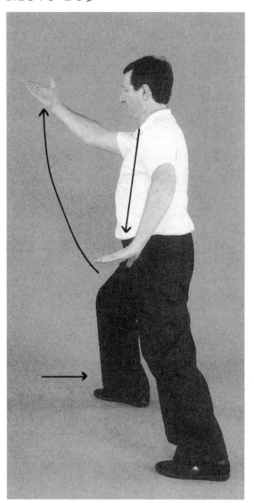

Fig. 141 *(Slanting flying right)* Move your right foot one step across to the south-west with your toes pointing south-east. As you shift your weight into a right forward stance, sweep your upturned right pal to the south-east and your left palm down by your left hip. Your right fingers are at eye level.

Move 166

Fig. 142 *(Slanting flying left)* Turn your right foot to the south. Move your left hand above your right knee and in line with your right hip. Turn your right hand over, placing it above your left hand. Take your left foot one step across to the north-east and shift into a left forward stance. Sweep your upturned left hand to the north-east and place your right hand by your right hip at the same time.

Move 167

Move 168

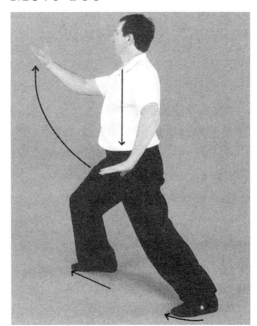

Fig. 143 Repeat move 164. You are facing north.

Fig. 144 ABOVE RIGHT Take half a step towards the south-east and repeat move 165.

Move 169

Fig. 145 Shift your weight on to your left foot in a snake stance and at the same time move your right palm to the north. Your right hand is in line with your left shoulder and directly above your left hand.

Move 170

Fig. 146 Shift 60% of your weight on to your right foot as you turn your body to the east. Both hands follow the turn of the body and your right wrist should hang down.

Move 171

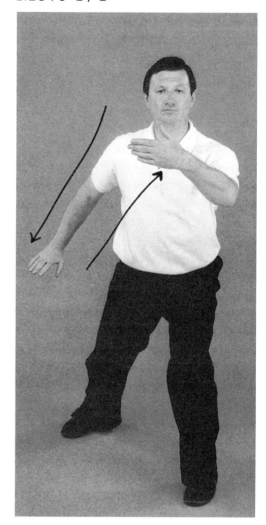

Fig. 147 Repeat move 8. To the north.

Move 172
Repeat move 9. To the east.

Move 173
Repeat move 10. To the east.

Move 174
Repeat move 11. To the east.

Move 175
Repeat move 12. To the east.

Move 176
Repeat move 13. To the east.

Move 177
Repeat move 14. To the east.

Move 178
Repeat move 15. To the north-west.

Move 179
Repeat move 16. To the south-east.

Move 180
Repeat move 17. To the north-west.

Move 181
Repeat move 18. To the west.

Move 182

Fig. 148 Move your left hand back over your left knee and transfer your right hand across in line with your left shoulder. At the same time, turn your left foot to the north. Your right hand should be directly above your left.

Move 183

Move 184

Fig. 149 Shift your weight on to your left foot and raise your right foot two inches from the ground. Turn your body and right foot to the north-east and rotate your left palm up as you do so. Place your right foot down with your weight still on your left leg.

Fig. 150 *(Fair lady plays at shuttles)* Shift your weight on to your right foot and turn your body to the east. Step to the north-east with your left foot. As you shift into a left forward stance, raise your left hand near your left temple and push your right hand to the north-east. Your right palm is at chest height.

Move 185

Fig. 151 Move 60% of your weight back on to your right toot. At the same time, move your right upturned palm above your right knee, in line with your right hip, and your left palm directly above your right palm. Your left hand is in line with your right shoulder and your body faces north-east. You are holding an imaginary ball.

Move 186

Fig. 152 Shift 60% of your weight on to your left leg as you -turn your body to the north. Your hands should follow the movement of your body and be positioned above your left leg. You are still holding the imaginary ball.

Move 187

Fig. 153 *(Fair lady plays at shuttles)* Shift your weight on to your left foot and sweep your right to the north-west - you have now turned through 270°. Move into a right forward stance, raising your right hand up near to the right temple and pushing your left palm towards the north-west.

Move 188

Fig. 154 Turn your left palm up and move it down above your right knee in line with your right hip. At the same time, transfer your right hand directly over your left palm and in line with your right shoulder. The two palms face each other, pointing in different directions. You are facing north-west with 60% of your weight on your right foot.

Move 189

Fig. 155 *(Fair lady plays at shuttles)* Move your left foot one step across to the south-west, with your toes pointing in the same direction. Transfer into a left forward stance, raising your left hand near your left temple and pushing your right palm to the south-west.

Move 190

Fig. 156 Transfer 60% of your weight on to your right leg and turn your body to the north-west. As you are turning your body, rotate your right hand up, move it down above your right knee and move your left hand in line with your right shoulder. This is a repeat of move 185.

Move 191

Fig. 157 Transfer 60% of your weight to your left leg and turn your body to the west. Your hand should follow the movement of your body and be positioned above your left knee. This is a repeat of move 186.

Move 192

Fig. 158 *(Fairlady plays at shuttles)* Shift all of your weight on to your left leg, turning your body and sweeping your right foot to the south-east. Transfer your weight into a right forward stance, raising your right hand near to your right temple and pushing your left palm to the southeast. This is a repeat of move 187.

Move 193

Repeat move 169.
To the north.

Move 194

Repeat move 170.
To the north.

Move 195

Repeat move 171.
To the north.

Move 196

Repeat move 9.
To the east.

Move 197

Repeat move 10.
To the east.

Move 198

Repeat move 11.
To the east.

Move 199

Repeat move 12.
To the east.

Move 200

Repeat move 13.
To the east.

Move 201

Repeat move 14.
To the east.

Move 202

Repeat move 15.
To the north-west.

Move 203

Repeat move 16.
To the south-east.

Move 204

Repeat move 17.
To the north-west.

Move 205

Repeat move 18.
To the west.

Move 206

Repeat move 94.
To the north.

Move 207

Repeat move 95.
To the north.

Move 208

Repeat move 96.

Move 209

Repeat move 97.

Move 210

Repeat move 98.

Move 211

Repeat move 99.

Move 212

Repeat move 100.

Move 213

Repeat move 101.

Move 214

Repeat move 102.

Move 215

Repeat move 103.

Move 216

Repeat move 104.

Move 217

Repeat move 105.

Move 218

Repeat move 106.

Move 219

Fig. 159 *(Snake creeps down)* Turn your right foot to the north-east and shift 90% of your weight on to your right foot and bend your knee. Your left hand points down near your left ankle. As you are moving down on to your right foot, turn your left foot in 45°, keeping the left knee slightly bent. Remain upright and only go as low as you feel is comfortable.

Move 220

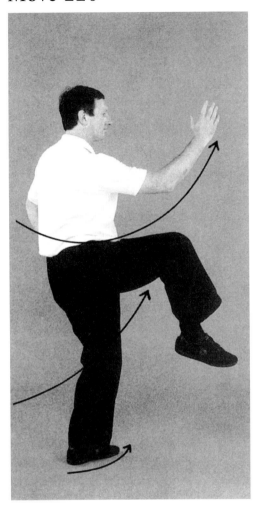

Move 221

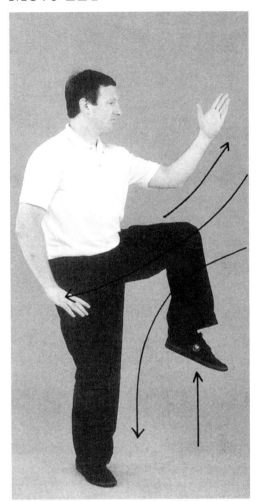

Fig. 160 *(Golden cock stands on one leg right)* Turn your left foot out to the south-west and shift yourself forwards on to it with the left hand still pointing down in front of you. Lift your right knee and right hand up at the same time to the west, as your left hand is pulled back by your left hip.

Fig. 161 *(Golden cock stands on one leg left)* Take one step back to the east with your right foot and move your right hand down by your right hip as you swing your left hand and left knee up.

Move 222

Fig. 162 Keep your left knee up and circle your right hand down and back to the east. As you are moving your right hand, turn your left palm up. The finger-tips of both hands should be at the height of the tips of your ears.

Move 223

Step back with your left foot to the east and repeat move 57

Move 224

Repeat move 58.

Move 225

Repeat move 59.

Move 226

Repeat move 60.

Move 227

Repeat move 61.
To the north-east.

Move 228

Repeat move 19 & 62.
To the north.

Move 229

Repeat move 20 & 63.
To the north.

Move 230

Repeat move 21 & 64.

Move 231

Repeat move 22 & 65.
To the north.

Move 232

Repeat move 23 & 66. To the north.

Move 233

Repeat move 24 & 67. To the west.

Move 234

Repeat move 25 & 68. To the west.

Move 235

Repeat move 26 & 69. To the west.

Move 236

Repeat move 70. To the west.

Move 237

Repeat move 71. To the west.

Move 238

Repeat move 72. To the west.

Move 239

Repeat move 73. Facing north.

Move 240

Repeat move 74. Facing north.

Move 241

Repeat move 75. To the east.

Move 242

Repeat move 76. To the east.

Move 243

Repeat move 77. To the east.

Move 244

Repeat move 78. To the east.

Move 245

Repeat move 79. To the east.

Move 246

Repeat move 80. To the east.

Move 247

Repeat move 81. To the east.

Move 248

Repeat move 82. To the east.

Move 249

Repeat move 83. To the north-east.

Move 250

Repeat move 84. To the east.

Move 251

Repeat move 10. To the east.

Move 252

Repeat move 11. To the east.

Move 253

Repeat move 12. To the east.

Move 254
Repeat move 13. To the east.

Move 255
Repeat move 14.

Move 256
Repeat move 15. To the north-west.

Move 257
Repeat move 16. To the south-east.

Move 258
Repeat move 17. To the north-west.

Move 259
Repeat move 18. To the west.

Move 260
Repeat move 94. To the north.

Move 261
Repeat move 95. To the north.

Move 262
Repeat move 96/208.

Move 263
Repeat move 97/209.

Move 264
Repeat move 98/210.

Move 265
Repeat move 99/211.

Move 266
Repeat move 100/212.

Move 267
Repeat move 101/213.

Move 268
Repeat move 102/214.

Move 269
Repeat move 103/215.

Move 270
Repeat move 104/216.

Move 271
Repeat move 105/217.

Move 272
Repeat move 106/218. To the west.

Move 273
Repeat move 107. To the west.

Move 274
Repeat move 108.

Move 275

Fig. 163 *(White snake pokes out its tongue)* Move your left foot forwards to the west. As you shift into a left forward stance, push your left fingers to the west and draw your right hand back near your elbow.

Move 276

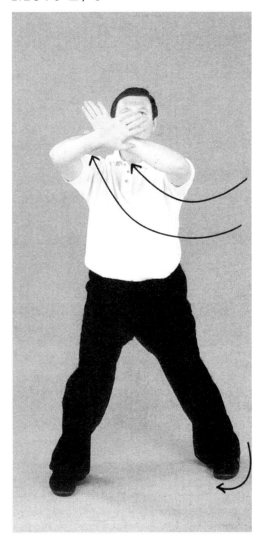

Fig. 164 Shift your weight back into a right snake stance. As you do so, turn both palms to the north and feel as if you are pushing up.

Move 277

Fig. 165 *(Lift knee and kick with heel)*
Move your weight back on to your left foot and make complete circles out and up with both of your hands. As you do so, lift your right knee and kick to the east.

Move 278

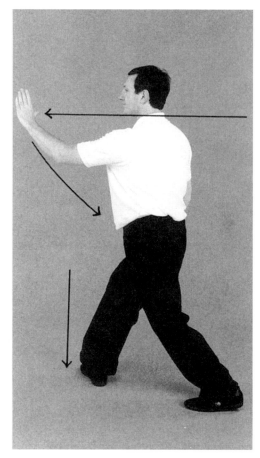

Fig. 166 *(Brush knee left)* Repeat move 121.

Move 279

Fig. 167 *(Step up and hit down)* Step to the east with your left foot and repeat move 122.

Move 282

Fig. 168 Repeat move 84. To the east.

Move 280

Repeat move 82.

Move 281

Repeat move 83. To the north-east.

Move 283

Fig. 169 *(Double hand grasp tail)* Repeat move 10.

Move 284

Fig. 170 *(Pull back)* Repeat move 11.

Move 285

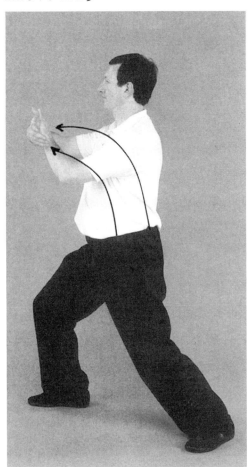

Fig. 171 *(Press)* Repeat move 12.

Move 286

Fig. 172 Repeat move 13.

Move 287

Fig. 173 *(Push)* Repeat move 14. To the east.

Move 288

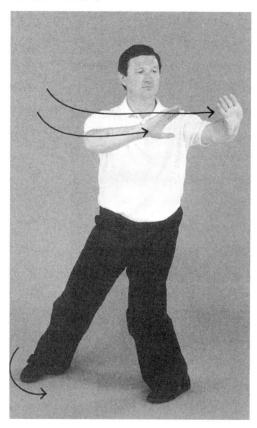

Fig. 174 *(Ward off to the left)* Repeat move 15. To the north-west.

Move 289

Move 290

Move 291

Fig. 175 *(Ward off to the right)* Repeat move 16. To the south-east.

Fig. 176 ABOVE RIGHT Repeat move 17. To the north-west.

Fig. 177 *(Single whip)* Repeat move 18. To the west.

Move 292

Move 293

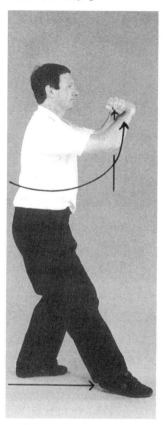

Fig. 178 *(Snake creeps down)* Repeat move 219. To the west.

Fig. 179 *(Step up to seven stars)* Turn your left foot south-west and step forwards with your right foot to the west in a cat stance. As you step forwards, swing your right fist up underneath your now closed left fist, to form a cross.

Move 294

Move 295

Fig. 180 *(Step back and ride the tiger)* **Next five moves** Step back with your right foot to the east and pull your hands eight inches (20 cm) apart, as if you are holding a ball. Your left heel is raised in a cat stance.

Fig. 181 ABOVE RIGHT Sweep your left and right hands out to the side simultaneously. Your left should be to the south and your right should point to the north. This move is similar to *crane spreads wings,* except the arms are spread wider.

Move 296

Fig. 182 Circle your hands in line with the centre of your body, with the left in front of the right.

Move 297

Fig. 183 Take a big step over to the east with your right foot, but leave your hands facing the west.

Fig. 184 ABOVE RIGHT Turn your body 180° to the right and allow your arms to swing around with the movement, to the west.

Move 298

Move 299

Fig. 185 Sweep both of your arms to the north, circle your right foot above and to the left of your left knee. Your left hand is in line with your right shoulder.

Move 300

Move 301

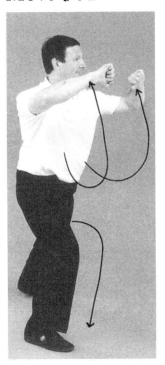

Fig. 187 Pull back your right foot, step to the north-west and sweep your hands upwards to the north-west.

Fig. 186 *(Slap foot)* Vigorously swing your right foot to the north and, at the same time, sweep your palms to the south to slap your foot. if you cannot lift your leg as high as illustrated, just lift it as high as you can and slap the leg. With practice you will be able to lift higher.

Move 302

Move 303

Fig. 189 Place your weight on your right foot and step over to the south with your left foot. Turn your body to the south and sweep both of your fists down and up to the south. Your fists are in line with your head.

Fig. 188 *(Bend the bow and shoot the tiger)* Turn your waist to the north as you push your left fist to the west.

Move 304

Fig. 190 Move your right foot half a step to the south and push your right fist back to the west.

Move 305

Fig. 191 Turn your right foot to the north-west, shift 80% of your weight on to your right foot and press your left palm to the west.

Move 306

Move 307

Fig. 192 *(Parry and punch)* Repeat move 38.

Fig. 193 ABOVE RIGHT Repeat move 39. To the west.

Move 308

Fig. 194 Repeat move 40. To the west.

Move 309

Move 310

Fig. 195 *(Close the door)* Repeat move 41. To the west.

Fig. 196 ABOVE RIGHT Shift your weight on to your right foot and turn your left foot in to form a snake stance, as you turn to face the north. As you move into the snake stance, open your hands slightly wider than the width of your shoulders. This is a repeat of move 42.

Move 311

Fig. 197 Shift your weight on to your left foot, in preparation for *cross hands*.

Move 312

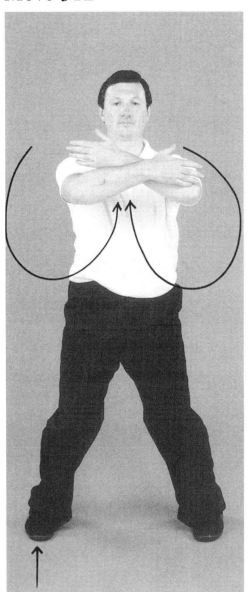

Fig. 198 *(Cross hands)* Shift your weight equally between your two feet, circling your hands down and up, crossing at the wrists as before.

Move 313

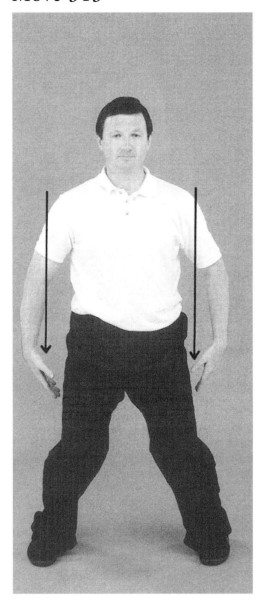

Fig. 199 Move your hands down by your hips.

Move 314

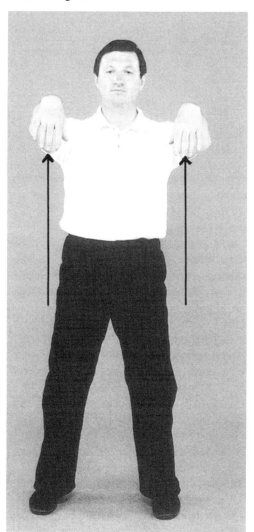

Fig. 200 *(Lift hands)* Straighten your knees and lift your hands to shoulder height.

Move 315

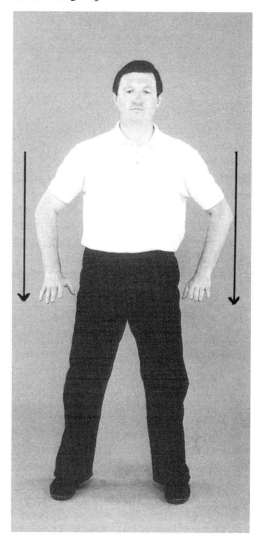

Fig. 201 Move your hands down by the side of your hips.

Finish

Pushing hands

The slow and gentle movements of the tai chi solo exercise are best known to students, but there are many other important aspects of the art. *Tui shou* or pushing hands is often considered as an intermediate step between the tai chi slow solo exercise form and tai chi self-defence training.

Pushing hands is practised with a partner and at first sight does not appear as appealing as the tai chi exercise form. But to exclude pushing hands from a balanced and complete training regime would be an error if you wish to benefit in all aspects of the art. Every facet of tai chi is contained within pushing hands practice.

Relaxation, correct posture, yielding, constant flow and the use of the whole body as a unit is intrinsic in its practice. The difference between pushing hands and the solo form is that in the former you are in physical contact with another person. Maintaining a good relaxed posture, a constant, unbroken flow, and a correct use of the body, becomes more difficult to achieve. This should act as a spur to every student - you will have to extend your present skills to encompass this new dimension to your training.

With practice, you will discover that you become 'as one' with your training partner. New faculties within you will be revealed as you are led to call upon hitherto latent abilities.

The main concept involved is called 'central equilibrium'- at all times during the exercise you must be in control of *all* your actions. This is exemplified in the maxim: *When one part moves, all parts move.* At all times your balance is central, directed by the centre within the waist. When pressing forwards the mind conceives the action and moves from the centre *(tan tien,* two inches below the navel), the back leg straightens, the front knee bends and the hands move straight ahead. When retreating in pushing hands, move the hands back and turn the waist, bending the back knee and straightening the front. Again, all actions are driven from the *tan tien* central point.

Posture

1   Hold the head as if suspended from above by a piece of string, tucking the chin in gently.

2   Your spine should be straight with the bottom gently tucked under.

3   Leave a gap of one fist width (approximately three inches) under the armpit. This will require you to hold your elbows away from your body slightly.

4   Relax your shoulders and let them hang down and slightly forwards.

5   Sink your breathing down to the *tan tien*.

6   Your knees should not go beyond the line of the foot.

7   Your knees should move forwards and backwards, **not** from side to side.

Single pushing hands

There are eight concepts which cover this first basic pushing hands exercise. They are: **Central equilibrium, Listening, Sticking, Yielding, Neutralising, Turning, Leading/ Following** and **Attacking.**

Central equilibrium

Explained earlier in this chapter (page 134).

Listening

Your mind should be free from extraneous thoughts and open to perceive the actions of your partner. Do not try to prejudge their actions. Feel their force through your sense of touch. Is it strong or weak? Is it coming in a straight line or slightly curved? Only by having an open mind that is listening can any distinctions be made.

When you first begin pushing hands, listen to your partner's force and movements without trying to influence the situation unduly. When you have attained sufficient skill in listening, you may begin to use the methods that follow, while still remaining subtle and 'open'. At all times you should be listening, both in attack and defence. Without listening you will not be able to respond, even to slight changes in attack or defence.

Sticking

During pushing hands practice, contact must be made *all* of the time. This is achieved by becoming sensitive and receptive to your partner's movements. When your partner presses forwards, you must move back at exactly the same speed, neither trying to get ahead or lag behind, simply acting like a mirror to their movement. If they turn to the left or right, you follow; when they move away, you stick to them.

Yielding

Once the partner has begun to push you, keep your arms firm but relaxed and start to move away in order to dissipate the forward energy. This is not a weak, empty motion, but a positive absorption of the attacking force in readiness to counter it.

The feeling of yielding is similar to that of a spring. When the spring is pushed in, it moves easily; but no matter how soft the spring, there is always a feeling of resistance present. Once the pressure on the spring is released, it immediately bounces out. The term 'soft yielding' is not 'soft' like a piece of cotton wool, but more akin to a spring or a piece of bamboo.

Turning

During pushing hands or self-defence applications, tai chi defence always encompasses a turn, no matter how small, in the defending movement. To oppose an oncoming force could easily unbalance you, but if you drop your centre of balance low and turn from the centre, you can deflect considerably larger forces than your own. Turning does not mean just from side to side, but also upwards and downwards. This idea is exemplified in the saying: *Four ounces defeats a thousand pounds.*

Neutralising

The term 'neutralise' can be understood on two levels in pushing hands practice. From a physical point of view, during practice the acts of yielding and turning together can be called neutralising - literally bringing your opponent's force against you to zero. This can be accomplished in many ways and to this purpose all of the pushing hands practice is aimed.

On another level, pushing hands *is* neutralising. All of the actions of pushing hands practice are directed at neutralising an oncoming force and, ultimately, at controlling and subduing it.

Leading/following

Once you have yielded and turned your partner, their flow of force should not be interrupted. By applying a small amount of force in the same direction, you may succeed in unbalancing them and placing them in a position where you can attack successfully.

Attacking

Once your partner's forward motion has been neutralised, their next movement will be backwards to regain balance. Stick to them and follow, applying your own attacking movement. No slack should be left, whether it is moving forwards, backwards or turning left or right.

Yin and Yang

All of the previous actions can be encapsulated in the Yin/Yang diagram *(see* fig. 1, page 13). The two sides of the diagram - one black (Yin) and the other white (Yang) - look like two fish entwined. You will note that the line dividing them is not straight but curved: this intimates that there is some forceful element (Yang) even within the passive receptive (Yin), and vice versa. Remember what was said previously about the spring-like quality of yielding - firm but soft. When attacking, the arm may be relaxed, but the movement contains hidden power, softness and strength - Yin within the Yang. This concept is easily understood when watching an explosive movement from the tai chi fighting form. Although the arm is relaxed, the body sends out explosive force meant to impart tremendous shocking energy. During this fixed step pushing hands, however, the force is hidden in the actions and softness and slowness are encouraged.

You will also note from the Yin/Yang diagram that the two fish's eyes are of the opposite colour, again emphasising the idea of the mixing process.

Pushing hands and the mind

During practice your mind should be receptive and clear, with no extraneous thoughts. Do not think about winning or losing, simply practise and 'feel' the exercise. The nearest experience to this state is the empty clarity of meditation, but in this instance you are in constant motion. The feeling of detached awareness, of being there but not being there, of moving with the motion rather than being the instigator of it, is very clear.

Investing in loss

The notion that you can gain by actually losing, or at least by being prepared to lose, may seem preposterous. But if you consider your own past experience you will find this is the case. When you have won at something in the past, did you sit down immediately and evaluate why you won? Did you ever consider that winning in that instance was good for you in the long term? Of course not: having been brought up in an era of 'winners and losers', it would seem unnatural. Investing in loss is intrinsic to pushing hands practice.

Yang Chien Hou is the man who exemplifies tai chi greatness. His behaviour is an example of investing in loss *(see* page 20). When asked how he had become so proficient in free-style pushing hands, he replied: 'I have lost one thousand times. I have lost ten thousand. But now I do not lose anymore. Each time I lost I learned. But I still followed the principles of not using strength but skill'. To defeat a greater physical force with skill takes time and practice. It will not come overnight.

The implied belief throughout tai chi teaching is that there is something of greatness within each human being, and that the training involved will allow this greatness to shine through without human interference. Lao Tsu, the great Taoist philosopher, said that we should be like a flowing river - soft and pliant, following the flow of the universe rather than opposing it. Tai chi exemplifies this teaching: when the flowing river meets an obstacle like a rock, it flows around it, over it and eventually through it. Nothing impedes its ever onward journey. Great is the force of water and its teaching.

The folowwing two pushing hands excercies are structured with each side knowing exactly what the other will do. These are known as **fixed step, pre-set pushing hands**. A pre-arranged excerise in which both sides move around is called **moving step, pre-set pushing hands**. When a two man drill is called **free-style**, each side may use whichever technique they wish within the prescribed rules.

The exercise centres around the use of the movement *ward off slantingly upward*. It is a single pushing hands exercise.

Fig. 202 Side *A* (on the left) is in a right back stance with her right palm touching the back of side *B*'s right hand. Side *B* (on the right) is in a front stance with his right arm extended, approximately 18 inches (45 cm) from his chest, and his palm facing his chest.

Fig. 203 *A* moves forwards, shifting her weight from her back foot on to the front foot and pushing with her right palm. *B* shifts his weight from his front foot on to the back foot, yielding as he moves his right hand back, mirroring *A*'s speed exactly. Remember: *A*'s right hand sticks lightly to *B*'s right.

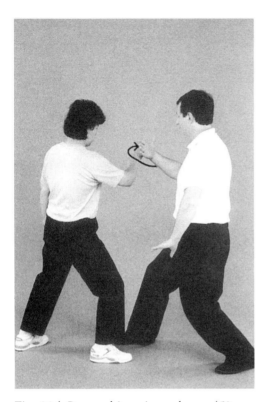

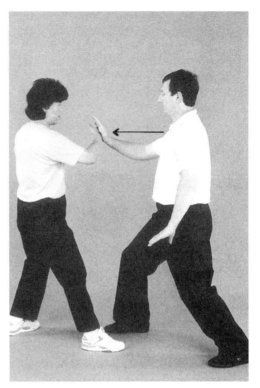

Fig. 204 *B* turns his waist and arm 45° to the right to neutralise the pushing action of *A*. Note: *B*'s right arm should never be less than 100° away from his body.

Fig. 205 Having neutralised *A*'s push, *B* turns his waist 45° to the left as he moves his weight into a right forward stance. *A* moves into a left back stance and moves her right arm back to mirror *B*'s forward push. Continue in this fashion with a constant flow of movement, each repeating the other's actions in turn. Also, remember to use the left side as well as the right.

Double pushing hands

When you can move freely and easily in single pushing hands, you can move on to the next stage - double pushing hands. This exercise is more complex than the previous one, but with practice should not prove too difficult.

You should now have the eight concepts - central equilibrium, listening, sticking, yielding, turning, neutralising, leading/following and attacking - under control. In the first exercise, the movement of using the back of your hand to hold off a push and to deflect to one side, before countering, is called *ward off slantingly upward*. To the seven concepts and the movement of *ward off slantingly upward (peng* in Chinese), we will add *pull back (lu), press (chi)* and *push (an)*.

Fig. 206 *B* stands in a right forward stance with his arms folded in front of his chest, his right hand touching his left elbow. *A* places her hands on *B*'s forearms near to the elbows and stands in a back stance.

Fig. 207 ABOVE RIGHT *A* moves forwards with *push (an)* in a right forward stance. *B* sits on to a right back stance, turning his waist 45° to the right *(turn right)*, and *wards upwards* as in figs 202 and 203 with his right arm. He holds *A*'s right wrist with his middle and ring fingers and sticks to *A*'s elbow with his left forearm.

Fig. 208 Immediately *A* pushes her right forearm forwards to *B*'s chest, with her left hand touching his right wrist - *press (chi)* - to neutralise.

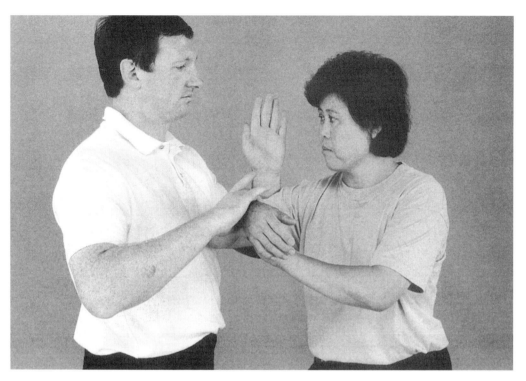

Fig. 209 The same movement from the other side, close up.

Fig. 210 To neutralise *A's press,* *B* turns his waist 45° again to the right to unbalance *A's* neutralisation.

Fig. 211 Once *B* has turned *A* to the right, he immediately moves into a right forward stance and applies *push (an)* - attack.

Fig. 212 *A* shifts into a back stance, allowing her right palm to touch her left elbow (as in fig. 205), and circles her left arm ready to catch *B's* right elbow (*lu*), as in fig. 206. *A* then performs the exact same movements of *B* previously, with *B* using *A's* former movements in a constant flow of motion. Therefore, the sequence will be: *A* uses *push; B* neutralises with *pull back; A* neutralises the *pull back* with *press; B* unbalances *A's press* and moves into *push; A* moves back and neutralises *B's push* with *pull back* before *B* would counter with *press,* and so on.

Free-style pushing hands

As has been previously stated, tai chi free-style pushing hands is an optional part of training. It will always be appealing to young people who are bursting with energy and who wish to put what they know into action. The practice also sharpens the reactions of those students of any age wishing to progress in the practical self-defence applications, putting theory into practice. With time and practice, middle-aged and older people can learn to neutralise and subdue their younger and stronger partners using the minimum amount of energy. But a considerable amount of dedicated pushing hands practice is necessary to achieve the sensitivity and skill required.

Please remember that you must have reached a competent level of skill in the fixed step, pre-set pushing hands exercises before you try free-style pushing hands. To begin the practice of free-style before acquiring relaxed skill will hamper your training. Once you have begun to use brute strength to achieve your goals in pushing hands it will be difficult to stop. Ultimately, this will hamper your progress in acquiring tai chi's soft skills.

There are two types of free-style pushing hands.

Free-style fixed step

In this competitive exercise, both players face each other in their on-guard stances. Any pushing, pulling or unbalancing tai chi technique may be used, but no striking or attacking of the face or vital areas is permitted. Each tries to force the other to lift or move their feet, thus scoring a point. During these competitive exercises, every technique of pushing hands will come into play, and the eight basic concepts have to be used effectively to prevent loss of balance and of points.

The use of the word 'competitive' in this instance should not be interpreted in the common sense, i.e. of avidly trying to defeat one another. It implies being more actively engaged with a training partner. Training sessions are always accompanied by a great deal of laughter and boisterous good humour, as both male and female students of all ages vie with each other. Students who do become too competitive tend to be the ones who are pushed and pulled all over the training area, much to their frustration. The more experienced and skilful, who have given up trying to win and have 'invested in loss', use the overt aggression of their partners to unbalance them and ultimately defeat them. Once frustration gives way to realisation that aggression alone will not succeed, the over-competitive student gives up competing and invests in loss. Age should not be a barrier: with practice the skill and sensitivity of constant training can allow older people to neutralise and subdue their younger and stronger partners. Like all aspects of tai chi, competitive pushing hands can be as gentle or as robust as you wish, to suit all ages and levels of ability.

Free-style free step

In free step free-style, throws, sweeps and freedom of movement are added to the fixed hand techniques. At the outset of free-style training, simply accept the fact that you will be thrown to the ground and be pushed out of the area. Accept it and know that by slowly learning the art you will ultimately gain great skill and fulfil your potential. Others will resort constantly to the use of physical strengthlet them. In the long term they will not succeed in these subtle skills. Invest in loss!

Rules

The following are rules observed by Hine Tai Chi Schools. Other associations and groups may have different rules.

1 A prescribed matted area 10-15ft (3-4½m) in diameter is to be used. Judo mats are the desirable medium.

2 The soles of the feet are the only part of each person's foot that is allowed to touch the ground. Any other part of the anatomy touching the ground will count as one point to the other person.

3 A person stepping out of the area will have one point awarded to their opponent. A person being pushed out of the area with one clean push will have two points awarded to their opponent. Relentless pushing to drive an opponent out of the area will not score.

4 Forbidden areas of the body to hold or grab in any way are the head, neck, groin and all joints.

5 Striking in any way is forbidden.

6 A throw will count as acceptable if it is completed successfully in one action; two or more attempts will not be allowed.

7 No contact with the torso is allowed during a throw, other than the arms or shoulders, which may touch the opponent's torso at any time. The thrower's leg may touch the other's leg during a contest in order to accomplish a throw.

8 Sweeping throws with the legs are acceptable as long as the sweep is accomplished at the first attempt. Unsuccessfully 'hacking' the leg is not acceptable.

9 The match should be conducted on the most friendly terms.

10 Forcing an opponent to the ground with brute strength will not score.

11 During a competition, a contest will last two minutes. In addition to the points scored with throws and pushes, a 'skill mark' will be awarded by the judge(s). (This skill mark will be out of **ten** points.) A competitor demonstrating very high levels of soft skill, executed with little external force and making total use of the opponent's force, will be awarded ten points. At the other end of the spectrum, a competitor who uses *only* brute strength, with no thought of skill or any of the stated principles of tai chi, will be awarded zero points. In between, one to nine points will be awarded accordingly.

(in reality, a skill mark of ten will rarely be given - this would indicate total perfection of tai chi skill. The skill mark is there to encourage competitors to use and acquire refined technique and to dissuade the use of brute strength and unrefined technique.)

Examples of free-style pushing hands

Example 1

Fig. 213 Partners *A* and *B* face each other, knees bent and at the ready. *A* is on the left in grey, *B* on the right in the white top.

Fig. 214 *(Pull back application)* *B* has observed that *A* has too much weight on his front foot while he is moving forwards. *B* catches *A*'s right wrist with his right hand and *A*'s right forearm with his left hand, and applies *pull back* to the right. *A* is jerked off his feet and his palm touches the ground. *B* scores one point.

Fig. 215 (*A* prevents *B's* successful *pull back* and moves away) *A* manages to escape from the *pull back* and begins to move backwards. *B* sees *A's* force moving away, steps forwards and applies *push* to hurl him out of the ring and score two points.

Example 2

Fig. 216 (*Brush knee* application) In the on-guard position. *B* takes a left foot forward stance.

Fig. 217 *A* places too much weight on his back leg. *B* swiftly moves forwards, catches *A*'s right leg behind the knee with his left hand, and lifts.

Fig. 218 Lifting *A*'s right leg unbalances him, and *B* applies a *push* to the chest. *A* falls inside the area, gaining *B* one point.

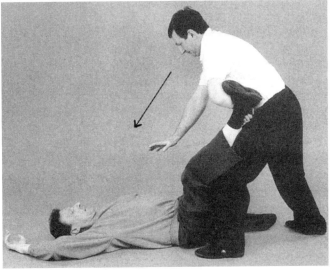

The examples above are just two of the hundreds of manoeuvres used within the free-style pushing hands arena.

Meditation

What is meditation?

Meditation is common throughout Asia. Tibet, China, Burma, India and Japan, along with many other nations, have amassed a vast expertise on the subject. But meditation has its roots in the West also. The forbearers of the Gnostics, a pre-Christian movement of some three thousand years ago, advocated very similar ideas to the Buddhists and Taoists in Asia. It is a common theme that 'Enlightenment', 'Cosmic Consciousness', 'Nirvana'- call it what you will - can be achieved only through meditation.

The Buddhist scriptures ('Sutras') state: *The mind is like a drunken monkey dancing on hot coals.* This is as true today as when it was written 2500 years ago. Our minds are in continual turmoil, hopping from one thing to the next, forever in motion. The unceasing chatter of our thoughts insulates us from reality. How can we possibly see anything in our lives with clarity while we are trapped between the past and the future?

The past is with us for much of the time; even though it has gone, it still impinges on the present. The nasty comments or deeds that have been done to us, even years earlier, still haunt and goad us. Anger, bitterness, regret and guilt are never very far away for most people. Life has a habit of amassing hurt; our minds are willing receptors as a place for this hurt to stay, ready to upset us once again.

The future, too, is an ever present uninvited guest - hopes, fears and day-dreams crowd in, filling the present and obscuring our lives.

The past is gone and will not return; the future has yet to come. Live in the now. This Buddhist verse states the obvious but wisdom is often *so* obvious that it eludes us. How many of us can say honestly that we live in the here and now, experiencing the present as it happens? Much of our day is missed as our minds are engaged in one pursuit after another. When we run out of those absolutely vital things we have to cram into our everyday lives, we invent new ones to fill our day - television, stereo, walkmans, DIY, and on and on. I am not saying that any of these are wrong or bad - far from it. But they often fill every passing moment of our free time, preventing us from seeing what is going on 'in here', not 'out there'. The whole of our lives are lived 'out there' - sights, sounds, smells, activity fill our consciousness. But what is happening 'here', inside of you, right now?

Modern Man has created an environment for himself which is totally alien to his nature. We live in little boxes, totally insulated from everything going on outside and from each other. We live in huge cities where we are crowded together, where tension and frustration abound. Co-operation and a common purpose have been replaced by excessive personal ambition and a 'Me first' attitude.

You may believe this to be true, but what can you do about it, just one person? The answer is meditation and tai chi. For a short time each day the senses will be turned in and the outside world excluded as you come face to face with your inner self.

Do not expect fast results; just practise without pre-conceived ideas as to what to expect. At first you may feel frustrated with your poor concentration, but persevere. Gradually you will find that meditation becomes easier. The chattering voice inside you will slowly subside and the peace will grow. A feeling of not being 'scattered', but whole, will eventually pervade you.

Meditation 1

Choose a quiet place that is clean and well ventilated. Be certain that for your period of meditation you will not be disturbed. Practise for 15 minutes in the morning and for the same at night, as a minimum.

Wear clean, loose fitting clothes, preferably for the sole purpose of tai chi meditation. Allow at least one hour after eating before commencing meditation or tai chi. Do not practise if you are upset or depressed and do not try to force yourself. Meditation should be a calming experience, not a traumatic one.

Do not lie down to meditate - you may fall asleep easily if you are too relaxed in your normal sleeping position. Either sit cross-legged in the lotus posture, or sit in a straight-backed chair. If you choose the latter, cross your legs at the ankles.

Before beginning the meditation proper, rub your two palms together vigorously for 30 seconds until they are very hot. Place one palm on your navel and circle the hand 81 times clockwise and the same anti-clockwise. Why 81? - tradition principally: within Taoism certain numbers are thought to have special significance and nine is one of these numbers. (Nine multiplied by nine is 81.) If you deviate and do 80 or 82 it would make no difference, but stick to the prescribed method as outlined. When you have completed the circling, your abdomen will feel warm inside as well as out. Keep your spine straight with your head held up slightly leaning forwards, but not too far. Relax your shoulders and hold your left thumb with your right hand. Rest your hands in your lap. (*See* fig. 219.)

Do not practise either of the two breathing meditations detailed here if you are pregnant or have a period.

Fig. 219 Meditation posture

Crane breathing

When you are seated comfortably, begin to feel the heat in the stomach at a point two inches below the navel on the inside - this point is called the *tan tien*. Relax the stomach: when you breathe in, allow the lower abdomen to *come out* gently. Do not force the breath. Allow it to be gentle and natural. Do not try to control it in any way. Before your lower abdomen reaches its maximum extension, apply slight tension to prevent it bulging.

When you breathe out, contract the abdomen to exhale the air. Remember, the movement of breath should be natural with no forcing in any way. Do not try to take deep breaths. Just quietly feel the abdomen for the prescribed length of time. When thoughts enter your head, just watch until they disappear and return to feeling the *tan tien*. Trying to force the thoughts to stay away will only make them proliferate. They will go if you watch them gently.

What can you expect to happen? Quite soon you will experience the heat in the lower abdomen simply by concentrating on the area. With practice you may experience a twitching sensation in the *tan tien*. This does happen often but do not be alarmed. Students have reported sleeping better and feeling stronger in themselves. Your breathing will become slower and deeper, without any manipulation on your part.

Zen Buddhist monks practise this particular exercise at the start of their meditation sessions each day. Do not underrate this meditation. Remember: *Enlightenment is about stripping away and making more simple, not more complex.*

Meditation 2

(Practise every day for at least three months before you add this following meditation.)

Use the same posture and breathing as before. On breathing in, visualise the air travelling from the nose down to the *tan tien*. On breathing out, visualise the air rising from the *tan tien* and taking the same path back up and out of the nose. Allow your breathing to move at its own pace - do not try to control it in any way. Practise for 15 minutes, morning and evening. Do not force the exercise.

Only practice can give you the benefits you require. The more consistent your training, the better the results. *One day's practice, one day's progress; one thousand days' practice, one thousand days' progress.*

Basically, what you put in is what you get out. If you have a choice between 15 minutes' deep, uninterrupted meditation daily, or one hour of intense meditation every three or four days, choose the former. Quality and regularity should be your watchwords. Slowly but surely your meditation will affect your thinking in everyday life. As you begin to take control of your days, it will strengthen your meditations. One should not be segregated from the other. The mind is the same in both instances; only the situations are different. The mind that races in everyday life is the same mind that sinks into tranquillity during meditation.

Perseverance is the most admired characteristic of the great masters in both East and West. It is what makes a master a master. When everyone else has given up, you are still there, fastidiously following the principles set out so long before. Come rain or shine you are following your quest. This is the secret of success in anything. Unfortunately, people still think they can buy it, or that there is a short cut to it. Once you have set out on your journey, do not be deflected - follow the road you have chosen to its end.

Chi kung

The ability to take in and store vital energy comes under the general heading of *chi kung*. There are hundreds of methods of *chi kung*, including Buddhist, Taoist and Confuscian sources in China. India and Tibet both had strong influences on *chi kung* in China. A great interchange took place between these countries, not only in trade, but also in culture and religious practice. Many Buddhist monks carried the teachings to China, and with them secrets of health and longevity. Since that time the Chinese have adapted and changed all that they have learnt, and produced the multi-faceted *chi kung* of today.

The main reasons for people performing *chi kung* can roughly be divided into three areas.

1 Health promotion/stress-free mind.

2 Longevity: *chi kung* advocates believe that correct and regular practice will ultimately lead to a healthy and extended life span.

3 Martial arts: the ability to generate tremendous power from *chi kung* training.

In *chi kung,* there are three requirements.

1 Mind: the mind must be calm and alert, with total concentration on the exercise.

2 Posture: throughout all of the different methods, posture must be correct.

3 Breathing: breathing is an integral part of *chi kung.* Some types emphasise the breathing in its length and duration; others do not. But even when it is not emphasised consciously, the breathing pattern is still changed markedly.

Where to practise

The best place to practise tai chi, *chi kung* and meditation is in the open air, surrounded by nature. Exercise near trees and where the air is pure and unpolluted. A quiet setting will be most conducive to practice. Training in the arts first thing in the morning will give you a wonderful start to the day. In the Far East, the parks are full just after dawn with people of all ages engaged in their various exercises.

If you are unable to practise outdoors, a well ventilated but warm room will serve well for your training area. At every opportunity make the most of any outdoor exercise.

The *chi kung* routine outlined below is called the 'Eight breathing *chi kung*'. It is a very popular method practised by both martial artists and health conscious individuals alike. It has proven over the centuries to be a most beneficial exercise regime for young and old. Its movements are straightforward and concise, dismissive of all flamboyant and superfluous motions. This makes an ideal exercise to be learned from a book. However, when the opportunity presents itself, take lessons from a competent teacher.

Eight breathing chi kung

Take each individual exercise and spend at least one week or more on each one. Start with four or five repetitions per exercise and work up to a maximum of ten. If at any one time during the *chi kung you* feel light-headed or queasy, stop immediately and rest. Only start again the following day, reducing the number of repetitions per exercise. Over the weeks, gradually build up to the maximum ten repetitions of each of the eight exercises. If you have to start on less than four or five reps, that is perfectly alright. Progress at your own speed: the destination is more important than the speed you get there. If you have any doubts about your health and ability to perform this *chi kung,* please consult your health advisor before commencing.

Use crane breathing throughout. Breathe naturally. Do not try to control the breathing in any way. Perform the exercise slowly and evenly.

Important
During each repetition on the in breath, send it down to the *tan tien*. On the out breath, imagine you are pushing against a heavy object of some sort **without tensing any of your muscles**. This will feel odd to begin with, but will soon be mastered. The reason this is done is to 'trick' the *chi* into flowing to the area. Visualising the body ready for hard work causes the energy to surge to the point of potential pressure. When it reaches the area and there is no *physical* activity, it will circulate to the skin of the fingers and palms. From the fingers it will move back into the body, having completed its circuit. The continual surging of the energy will cause the *chi* flow not only to grow stronger, but to circulate throughout the whole body. The extra vital energy circulation will encourage the repair of cells and the removal of waste, revitalising the system in general and strengthening the flow to the extremities. If you are a martial artist, this increase in *chi* to the legs and hands will increase power in your strikes.

Excercise 1

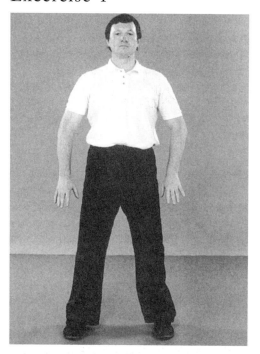 

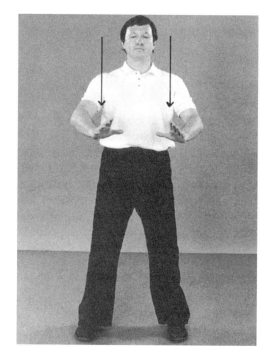

Fig. 220 *(Lift hands)* Stand relaxed, spine straight, head up, with your feet parallel and one shoulder width apart. Your hands hang by the sides.

Fig. 221 ABOVE RIGHT As you breathe in, slowly lift your hands in front of you, wrists uppermost and fingers hanging down. By the time you have completed your in breath, your hands should be in line with your shoulders

Fig. 222 Move your hands as if pressing down on something, breathing out as you do so. Your hands should end up by your sides as in fig. 219. Repetitions: start with four and slowly work up to ten.

Excercise 2

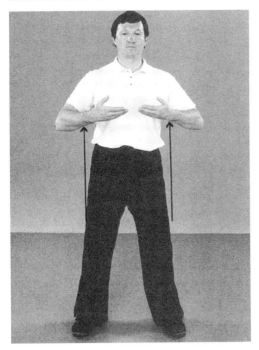

Fig. 223 *(Holding up the sky)* ABOVE LEFT From the starting position (fig. 220), lift your hands, palms up, to chest height as you breathe in.

Fig. 224 ABOVE Turn your palms up and slowly push upwards as you are breathing out.

Fig. 225 With your palms still pointing up, slowly move them down to face level as you are breathing in. Turn your hands over so that your palms face down. As you are breathing out, press your palms down as in fig. 222. Repetition: as in exercise l.

Exercise 3

Fig. 226 *(Separate the hands)* RIGHT Begin as in fig. 220. Slowly lift your hands with your palms facing each other, as if you are holding a ball, your left palm on top, your right underneath, breathing in as you do.

Fig. 227 FAR RIGHT Slowly push your left palm up and your right palm down in a straight line, as if you are pushing against something, breathing out as you do so.

Fig. 228 RIGHT Slowly return your hands to the hold-the-ball position, breathing in as you do so.

Fig. 229 FAR RIGHT Slowly push your right palm up and your left palm directly down, breathing out. Move your hands back to the hold-the-ball position, breathing in. You have now completed one repetition (fig. 226). Repetitions: as in exercise 1.

Exercise 4

Fig. 230 *(Separate the hands diagonally)* FAR LEFT Start as in fig. 220. Move your hands up to the hold-the-ball position, breathing in.

Fig. 231 LEFT Slowly push your left palm diagonally up to the left and your right palm diagonally down to the right, breathing out.

Fig. 232 FAR LEFT Return your hands to the hold-the-ball position, breathing in.

Fig. 233 LEFT Slowly push your right palm diagonally up to the right and your left palm diagonally down to the left, breathing out. You have now completed one repetition.
Repetitions: as in exercise 1.

Exercise 5

Fig. 235 Turn your palms out and slowly push to the sides, breathing out.

Fig. 234 *(Pushing out to the sides)* Start as in fig. 220. Slowly lift your hands, palms up, to chest height, breathing in.

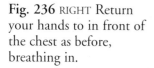

Fig. 236 RIGHT Return your hands to in front of the chest as before, breathing in.

Fig. 237 FAR RIGHT Turn your palms over and slowly press your hands down, breathing out. You have now completed one repetition. Repetitions: as in exercise 1.

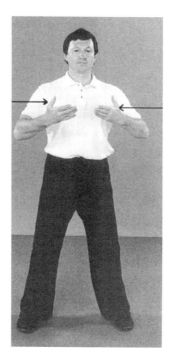

Exercise 6

Fig. 238 *(Pushing to the front)* RIGHT Start as in fig. 220. Slowly lift your hands, palms up, to chest height, breathing in.

Fig. 239 FAR RIGHT Slowly push your palms forwards, breathing out.

Fig. 240 RIGHT Slowly return your hands to in front of your chest, breathing in.

Fig. 241 FAR RIGHT Slowly press your hands down, breathing out. You have now completed one repetition. Repetitions: as in exercise 1.

Exercise 7

Fig. 243 Slowly press your hands down in front of yourself, breathing out. You have now completed one repetition. Repetitions: as in exercise 1.

Fig. 242 *(Circle inwards)* Begin as in fig. 220. Slowly circle your hands, palms up, out to the sides and above your head, breathing in.

Exercise 8

Fig. 244 *(Circle outwards)* Begin as in fig. 220. Slowly circle your hands, palms facing your body, inwards and upwards, above your head, breathing in.

Fig. 245 Continue to slowly circle out to the sides and downwards, breathing out. You have now completed one repetition. Repetitions: as in exercise 1.

If possible, practise every day, preferably before the tai chi solo form. Remember to leave at least one hour before eating and any exercise. Do not try to control your breathing: perform the exercise at the speed which feels comfortable to you. Do not try to fill your lungs to capacity: allow your breathing to find its own depth.

Self-defence applications

The principle difference between tai chi self-defence and virtually all other martial arts is the notion of 'non-contending'. By this I mean not opposing the oncoming attack with force. The normal reaction for most people would be to block the oncoming attack with all that they could muster. Tai chi, on the other hand, would try to dissipate the force with a light parry, or to dodge the attack altogether. When a blow has been thrown at full force and misses, it will leave the attacker unbalanced. During this unbalanced time, the tai chi exponent would attack and try to make the most of any weaknesses in the other's defence. It is at this point that tai chi would try to take control with pushing hands sensitivity. All of the principles of pushing hands would come into play.

Central equilibrium is maintaining your own balance and controlling that of the attacker, co-ordinating the movements in attack and defence of the four limbs with that of the centre. If this can be applied effectively with all of the techniques, the greatest possible amount of force can be generated.

Sticking at close range will allow you to feel what is potentially coming. This is not magic- when the hands become ultra sensitive to movement, a good level of interpreting can take place. When a person begins to move forwards, it is preceded by a change in balance which is quite discernible with practice. If the forward motion is a lunge, the tai chi practitioner would attempt to use the force by sticking, yielding, turning (neutralising) and applying some force of their own. A backward shift of weight might indicate a kick off of the front leg is coming. In this instance it would be correct to move into the position of weakness that has been created by the move, so that as the antagonist moves backwards, the tai chi practitioner will move forwards and apply force against the other's body. This is covered in the classical tai chi saying: *When he retreats, follow.* Again, in this instance the other person's force is used against them, plus the added tai chi force.

When you are pulled, do not try to resist with force - stick and neutralise by body turning while controlling the hands and legs (at which point the use of the shoulder, elbow or throwing technique might be in order). These are just a few of the situations and responses that might be applied in a given situation. There are literally hundreds of tai chi responses to any given technique.

Neutralising is applied in practical self-defence before a person can use force or after the force has been yielded to. When someone lifts their hand above their head to strike down at your own head, move in close and at the same time lift up your arm to the attacker's elbow to jam it. If this is applied correctly and timed well it will lead to them falling backwards. Very little force is needed to accomplish this. The example just alluded to is a matter of neutralising before force can be applied.

To apply neutralising after yielding can be illustrated when someone gives you a big two-handed push. Stick to them, yield on to your back leg, and turn the waist (centre) to neutralise to the left or right. (We sometimes refer to this as 'creating holes'.) To apply force to an apparently resisting object which then suddenly disappears will cause you to fall forwards. This is akin to walking on solid ground which suddenly gives way as you step into a covered hole. You come down hard on to that leg and for a few moments you are unable to recover. Hence the name.

Attack with any tai chi technique when the assailant is unbalanced. This can be at any moment, but remember to stick with one hand as you apply the attacking strike with either hand or foot. Your attack may not finish the conflict and you will have to be in a position to control whatever happens afterwards, be it attack or defence.

Solo application training

Training without a partner is most important. During this period the integration of all the concepts learned should be applied. Moving from your centre, co-ordinating hands and feet, and maintaining good balance should be at the forefront of your thinking. Initially the training should be conducted slowly and carefully, concentrating on each point. Once you can move smoothly and easily through each manoeuvre, start to visualise an opponent in front of you, throwing punches or kicks to the appropriate techniques. Do not apply muscular force: when your movements are smooth and well balanced, force will begin to appear.

Jing

Jing is concentrated force, developed from the combination of chi *kung,* solo form and training application. When they are all taken together and combined with will and intention, *Jing* can be produced.

Jing is an explosive surge of energy which takes time and a great deal of training to produce. But the amount of energy derived can be quite spectacular. When *Jing* is used the body is totally relaxed before the release of energy. At the moment of release, the body explodes into activity for a fraction of a second, with the attention focused on one small striking point. This striking point may be on the hand, foot or any part of the body. Once the energy is delivered, the body returns to a state of complete relaxation. The closest analogy of *Jing* is that of a bomb exploding. At one moment there is no sign of any motion or activity, the next tremendous force has been unleashed in a split second.

When you have acquired skill in the self-defence technique and the use of *Jing*, you may move through the applications using explosive force. Remember to relax before and immediately after the technique. Apart from the more obvious advantages of using explosive force in training, stamina and endurance are also developed. If you are using self-defence application training as part of your regular routine, practise the self-defence manoeuvres *before* you practise the solo slow form.

Fig. 246 *(Ward* off *slantingly upward) A* attacks with a left punch to the head. *B* parries with his right arm, while his left arm guards his body. His weight is on his right leg.

Fig. 247 *B* steps forwards with his left leg and strikes *A*'s neck with the edge of his left hand.

Applications

On the left is man *A*, who is the attacker. On the right is man *B*, who is the defender.

Fig. 248 *(Pull back) A* attempts to catch *B*'s shirt with his left hand.

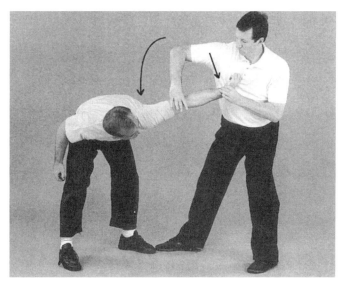

Fig. 249 *B* catches *A*'s left wrist with his left hand and applies pressure behind *B*'s left elbow.

Fig. 250 *(Press)* If *A* manages to pull away from the previous technique . . .

Fig. 251 . . . *B* leaps forwards and hits *A* in the chest with a forward elbow strike.

Fig. 252 *(Push) A* tries to grab *B* by the collar with his left hand.

Fig. 253 *B* turns to his left, pushing *A*'s left arm to the left, and applies a powerful push to the shoulder.

Fig. 254 *(Crane spreads wings/brush knee) A* punches with his right fist to *B*'s body, and then strikes to *B*'s head with his left fist. *B* parries low with his left hand and high with his right.

Fig. 255 *B* strikes back with a palm strike to the face.

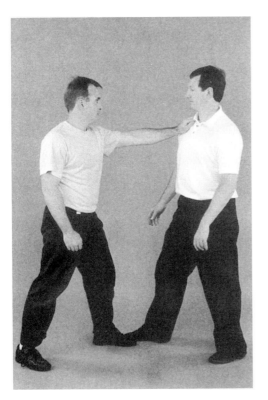
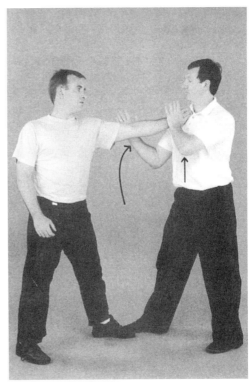

Fig. 256 *(Raise hands play the lute) A* catches *B*'s collar with his left hand.

Fig. 257 *B* catches *A*'s left wrist and immobilises it, then jerks his right palm against *A*'s elbow.

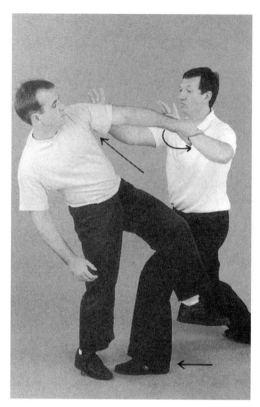

Fig. 258 *(Close the door)* A catches B's left wrist with his left hand. B twists the catch with his left hand.

Fig. 259 B steps forwards with his left foot and delivers a powerful push to A's shoulder, pinning his arm against his body and toppling him over.

Fig. 260 *(Parry and punch) A* punches at *B's* face with his left fist.

Fig. 261 *B* parries the punch with his right palm and delivers a straight punch with his left fist to *A's* solar plexus.

Fig. 262 *(Carry tiger to the mountain) A* swings a kick into *B's* mid-section. *B* side-steps, parries down to the right and covers the kick with his left hand.

Fig. 263 *B* steps forwards and throws *A* backwards.

Fig. 264 *(Holding up the sky)* A attempts to chop B from above with his left hand. B parries upwards with his left hand.

Fig. 265 B delivers a powerful right sweeping kick to the outside of A's left leg.

Fig. 266 *(Fist under the elbow)* A swings a right hook to B's head. B parries with his left hand.

Fig. 267 B strikes in an upward motion to A's ribs.

Fig. 268 *(Repulse monkey)* A tries to grapple with B; B parries A's right arm with his left forearm.

Fig. 269 B hooks his right foot behind A's right ankle, pulling it up and pushing A with his right palm.

Fig. 270 *(Part the wild horse's mane)* A punches to B's head with his left fist. B turns to the left and parries with his left arm.

Fig. 271 B steps behind A's left leg with his right leg and sweeps his right arm across A's neck.

Fig. 272 *(Wave hands like clouds)* A throws a right punch to B's head. B parries with his left forearm while sweeping across with his right arm to protect his body.

Fig. 273 B steps in and strikes A in the face with the edge of his right hand.

Fig. 274 *(Embrace the tiger)* A throws a straight right at B who parries with his left forearm to the right.

Fig. 275 B sweeps A's right arm away and strikes with a right hook to A's head.

Fig. 276 *(Ying Yang hand/Parry down and hit with fist)* A attempts to grab B's shirt with his right hand. B parries to the left with his left forearm and strikes A's face with a back fist.

Fig. 277 Before A can recover, B strikes with his left palm heel to A's face.

Tai chi double-edged sword form

The tai chi double-edged sword is called the *chien* and is described as the king of the short weapons. A thorough knowledge and expertise in the tai chi solo form should have been gained before moving on to this sophisticated weapon. Without the knowledge and expertise empty handed training can give, the wielder of the sword will appear clumsy and lifeless.

The sword should be looked upon as an extension of the solo tai chi form outlined in this book. Once the student can guide the *chi* effortlessly to the fingers, feet and throughout the body, the next step is to extend it further. To achieve this, tai chi uses four weapons - double-edged sword, broadsword, staff and lance.

The blade of the sword is flexible to facilitate the movement of energy along its length. When the sword is thrust forwards and the energy directed to its tip, a discernible wave of force should travel along its body. But a sword, especially a good one, is very expensive and many people practise with a wooden one instead. Although it lacks the great flexibility of the spring steel sword, great progress can still be made in strengthening the *chi* with it.

The principles governing the use of the sword are the same as with the solo form and pushing hands. Central equilibrium, sticking, neutralising, leading and attacking are all part of its application. Leading is an extension of neutralising and involves leading your partner or assailant into a position where you may attack and score. Control is the watchword of leading when you move from the defensive cycle of sticking and neutralising to that of attacking.

Hine Tai Chi Schools uses three Chien forms. The form demonstrated here is called the 'small idea sword', which contains all the basic elements necessary for successful use. It should not be considered as a beginner's form which is inferior to the other two, more as a vital first step without which skill and dexterity could not be gained. The small idea form is akin to learning the alphabet - without it words, sentences and paragraphs could not be constructed. Many of the postures learned in this form are repeated in the later forms in their more advanced stages.

Once the solo *chien* forms can be performed with dexterity, two-man exercises can be learned. Among these are routines called 'sticky swords', similar in many respects to pushing hands. At the beginning of sticky swords, partners touch their swords together and move through pre-set manoeuvres to develop sensitivity and finesse. At no time are the students allowed to break the connection between the two swords.

For the purpose of these two-man exercises, wooden swords are used for safety. 'Free-style sticky swords' is an extension of the earlier two-man exercises, differing in the sense that you may attack or defend in any way you wish. To break contact in order to score a point would place you in a position where you could be scored upon through lack of contact. This free-style exercise is not only very instructive, but also great fun. All of the techniques learned can be put into action, and all of your acquired skills honed in safety.

Beyond sticky swords are two-man pre-set routines, or *san shou,* and two-man free-style sparring. The *san shou* are directly derived from the solo form in which two people run through known attack and counter-attack without deviating from the pattern. In free-style sword sparring, the two training partners attempt to 'cut' the partner's wrists with their wooden swords. Again, all of the principles must be applied in this free flowing exchange of techniques. At no time is any other part of the body to be attacked apart from the wrists. Sticking and leading are very important to this form of tai chi training, together with the complex of footwork patterns employed. At all times safety should be the priority: wild flailing techniques are not allowed.

Sword form

Rules for practice

The rules governing the tai chi sword are basically the same as for the empty hand solo form detailed earlier. The difference between the sword and the empty hand forms is that of speed. In the sword form you will tend to move somewhat faster than in the solo form. This does not mean that you move so fast that you start to pant and breathe hard. Your movements should be smooth and relaxed, with light and agile movements of the feet.

Integrate the actions of the arms and legs, blending them together like pearls on a necklace, separate movements in continual, integrated flow. The sword will seem clumsy and unwieldy initially, making it difficult to use. But with steady practice the implement will become part of you, an extension of your will.

To learn the form well, be consistent and practise every day, even if it is for a few minutes only. Take one posture at a time and exercise until you can perform its actions with smoothness and accuracy, before moving on to the next posture.

The sword charm

The free hand that is not wielding the sword is just as important as the one that is, with regard to the point of *chi* circulation and the balance of the form. When the sword arm moves out in an expansive movement, the other hand moves out to balance the action, encouraging a flow of energy down the sword arm. When the sword arm shifts back in towards the body, the supporting arm also reciprocates the action, as a general rule.

The 'sword charm' is the name given to the free hand which is held as in fig. 278. The small and ring fingers are folded over, with the thumb resting on them; the middle and index fingers are held straight. The configuration of the sword hand is believed to encourage the flow of *chi* during the exercise.

We will again use the points of the compass to indicate the direction in which you should be facing. At the beginning of the form you are facing north.

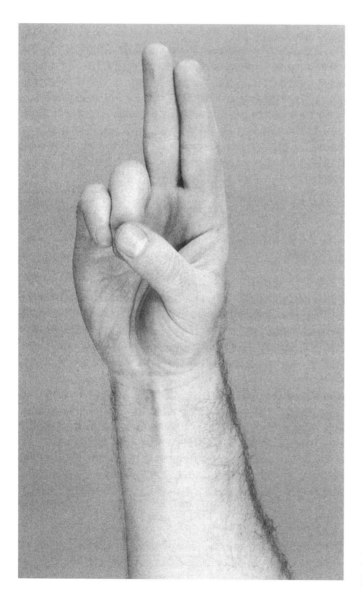

Fig. 278 'Sword charm' position of free hand

The small idea sword form
Move 1

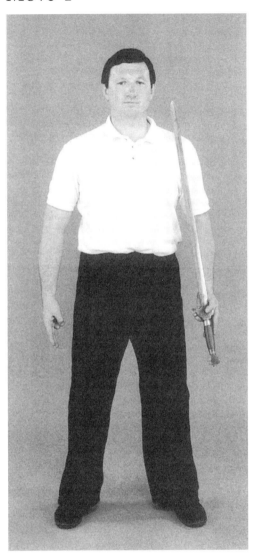

Fig. 279 *(Opening)* Stand with your feet one shoulder width wide. The hands hang by the sides with the palms facing forwards.

Move 2

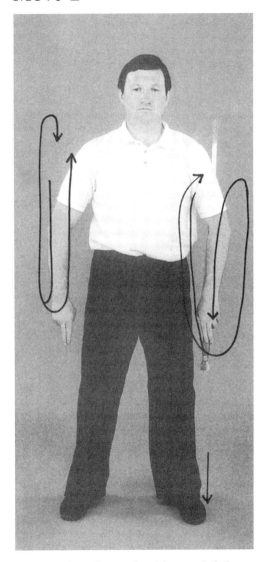

Fig. 280 Step forwards with your left foot and raise your hands in front of you to shoulder height. Move your right foot parallel to your left and at the same time circle your hands forwards 360°. The sword is now behind your left arm.

Move 3

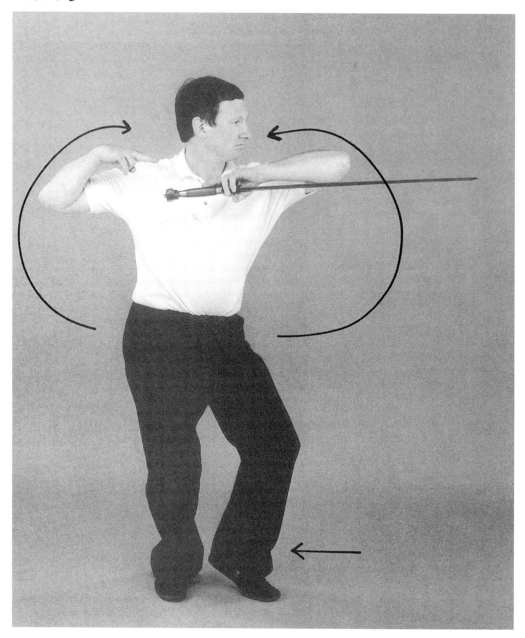

Fig. 281 *(Bend down on one leg)* Circle your left hand out to the left, stopping in front of the chest, and bend your knees. Immediately circle the right hand out to the right and finish with the fingers pointing towards the sword hilt.

Move 4

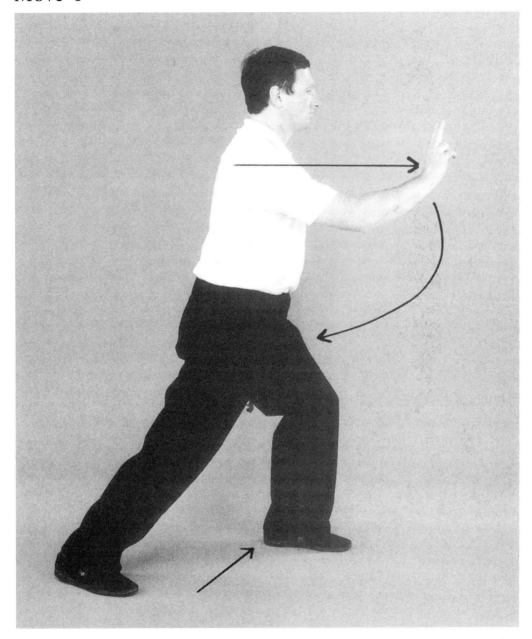

Fig. 282 *(Point the way)* Take a step to the west with your left foot, move into a forward stance and point the right fingers to the west. The sword hilt is at your left hip.

Move 5

Fig. 283 Turn your left foot out, stepping forwards with your right foot and circling the sword back, upwards and forwards to touch your right wrist.

Move 6

Fig. 284 Turn out your right foot and circle your right hand back. Step forwards with your left foot and touch the back of your left hand with your right fingers.

Move 7

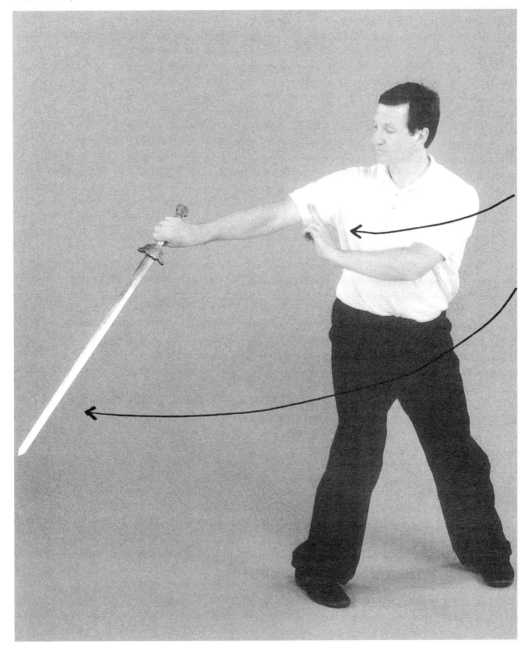

Fig. 285 Grasp the sword handle with your right hand and sweep the sword down and back towards the east, as you move into a snake stance. Your left hand moves in towards the chest.

Move 8

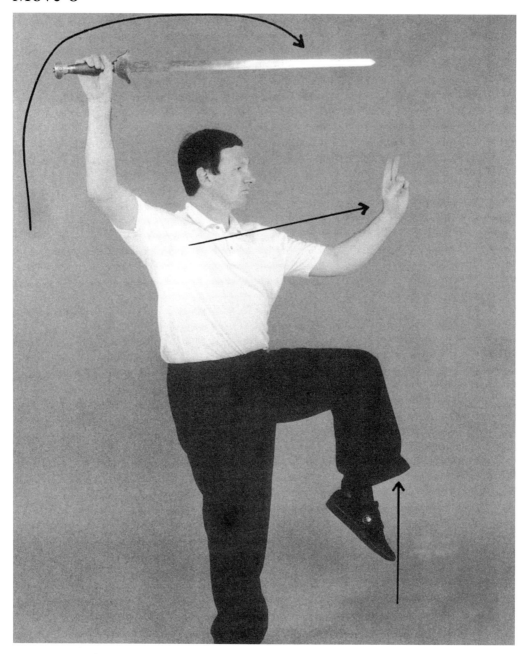

Fig. 286 *(Big dipper)* Continuing the previous action, circle the sword up and to the west, finishing above your head. At the same time move your left hand to the west and raise the left leg.

Move 9

Fig. 287 *(Sweep downwards)* Circle the sword down and up towards the west in a forward stance. Your left fingers touch your right wrist.

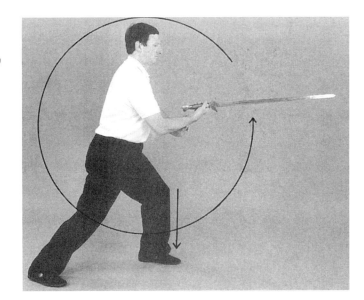

Move 10

Fig. 288 *(Intercept to the right)* Turn your left foot out to the left, shift your right foot forwards one step and circle the sword to the right.

Move 11

Fig. 289 *(Intercept to the left)* Turn your right foot to the right, take a step forwards with your left foot and circle the sword to the left.

Move 12

Fig. 290 *(Little dipper)* Take a step to the north-west with your right foot. Sweep the sword downwards and up to the north-west, lifting your left knee. Your left hand is placed behind the sword, which is at a 45° angle.

Move 13

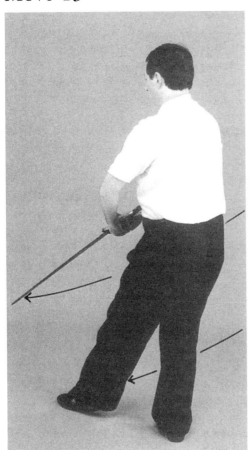

Fig. 291 *(Swallow enters the nest)* Place the left foot down to the south-east, behind your right foot. Turn your body to the left and press down your sword at a 45° angle.

Move 14

Fig. 292 *(Lively cat catches a mouse)* Flip the sword up and simultaneously lift your right foot to the south-east.

Move 15

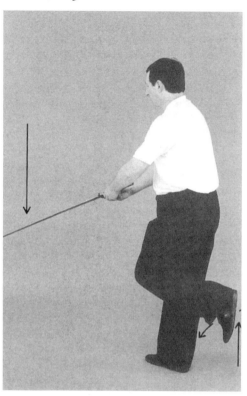

Fig. 293 *(Horse leaps the stream)* Place the right foot down one step towards the south-east. Allow the sword tip to drop downwards and lift the left foot.

Move 16

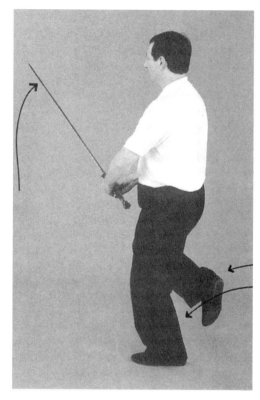

Fig. 294 Hop from the right foot on to the left foot, one step towards the south-east. As you hop, allow the sword to bob up with the spring of the body.

Move 17

Fig. 295 *(Insert the sword obliquely down)* Take one step forwards with your right foot and push your sword down at a 45° angle.

Move 18

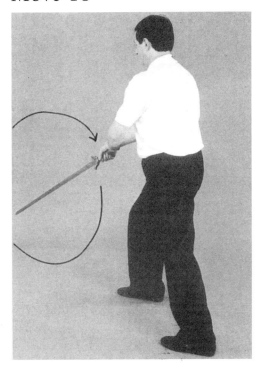

Fig. 296 Circle the left hand out to the left and down to touch the wrist with your left fingers.

Move 19

Fig. 297 *(Chop up and down) Flip* the sword tip upwards at a 45° angle and allow it to drop back to its original position. Repeat a second time.

Move 20

Fig. 298 *(Enter the cave)* Turn your right foot out 45°, take one step forwards with your left foot and insert the sword down at a 45° angle.

Move 21

Fig. 299 *(Phoenix spreads its wings)* Release your grip with your left hand and swing your right foot one step behind your left to the north-west. Shift your weight on to your right foot and sweep the sword to the north-west as your left hand swings towards the south-east.

Move 22

Fig. 300 *(Little dipper)* Sweep your sword back past your left shoulder, turn your right foot out 45° and lift your left knee towards the north-west. At the same time, the sword should arc up with the action of the knee. The sword should finish at an angle of 30° from the vertical, with your left fingers behind it.

Move 23

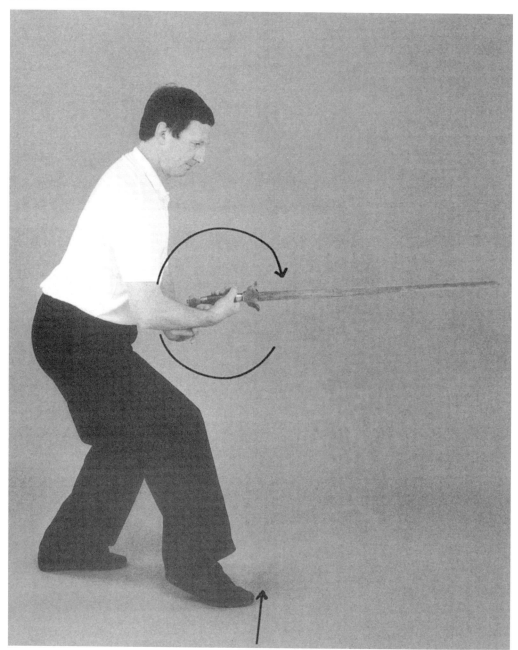

Fig. 301 *(Cut with back of sword)* Move your left foot one step back to the south-east and slide your right foot back into a cat stance. At the same time as you move the right foot, circle the sword back and chop down towards the west.

Move 24

Fig. 302 *(Winnowing the grass)* Move your right foot forwards, touch your right wrist and move the sword outwards to the right. You are in a forward stance.

Move 25

Fig. 303 Turn your right foot out, step forwards with your left foot one step and move the sword to the left.

Move 26

Fig. 304 Turn your left foot out, step forwards and repeat move 24.

Move 27

Fig. 305 Shift your weight on to your left foot, in a cat stance, as you circle the sword to the left, ending in line with the centre of your body.

Move 28

Fig. 306 *(The bird flies up)*
Make a small anticlockwise circle with your sword and immediately lift the left knee and thrust the sword to the west. As you thrust the sword, lift your left hand near the temple.

Move 29

Fig. 307 Place your left foot back one step to the east and shift your weight into a cat stance. As you shift your weight back, circle the sword to the right and touch your right wrist with your left fingers.

Move 30

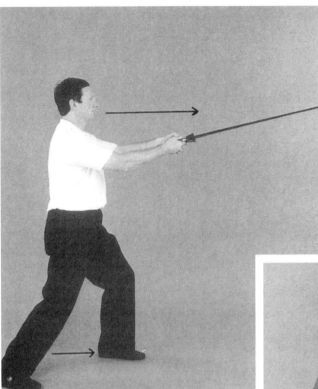

Move 31

Fig. 308 *(Dragon skims the water)* Turn your right foot out, step forwards with your left foot and thrust the sword forwards.

Fig. 309 *(Wind rolls the lotus leaf)* Turn your body to the right and sweep your sword to the east as you shift into a snake stance.

Move 32

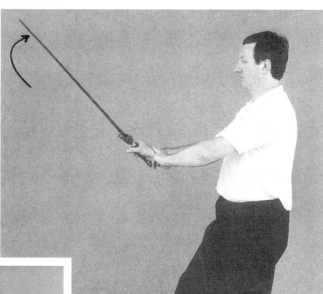

Move 33

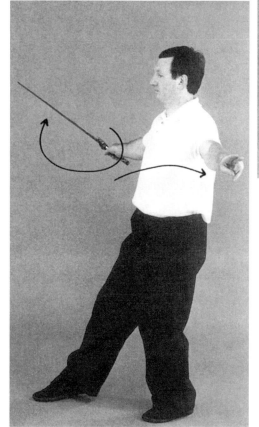

Fig. 310 ABOVE As you shift into a cat stance, make a small clockwise circle with the sword to the right.

Fig. 311 LEFT Spread the left hand and the sword out to the left and right simultaneously.

Moves 34/35/36/37

(Horse leaps the stream)
Repeat moves 15/16/17/18.
To the east.

Move 38

Move 39

Fig. 312 *(Turn and pull the horse)* Turn your body to the left and sweep the sword to the west as you move into a snake stance.

Fig. 313 Shift your weight back into a cat stance and pull the sword in towards you.

Move 40

Fig. 314 *(A compass point)* Take your right foot forwards one step parallel to the left, one shoulder width wide. As you do so, thrust your sword directly forwards.

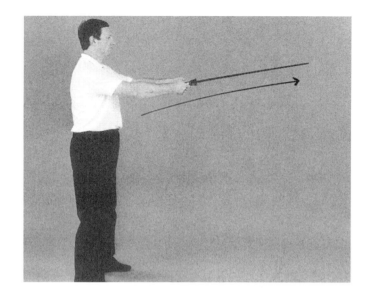

Move 41

Fig. 315 Make a small half-circle of the sword to the right.

Move 42

Fig. 316 *(Intercept to the left)* Take one step forwards with your left foot and perform move 12. To the west.

Move 43

Repeat move 10.
To the west.

Move 44

Repeat move 11.
To the west.

Move 45

Fig. 317 *(Drifting with the current)* Shift your weight on to the right foot, in a snake stance, and sweep the sword to the north.

Move 46

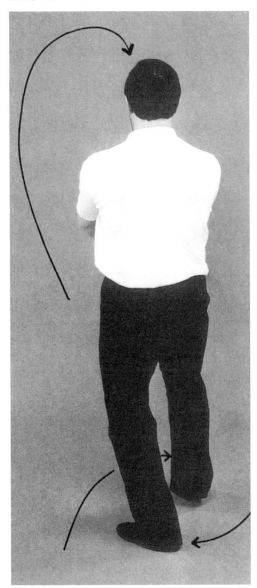

Fig. 318 *(Chop down)* Take one step towards the north with your left foot, turn your body to the right, circling the sword up, and chop down to the south. As you turn your body, move your right foot across to the west one step.

Move 47

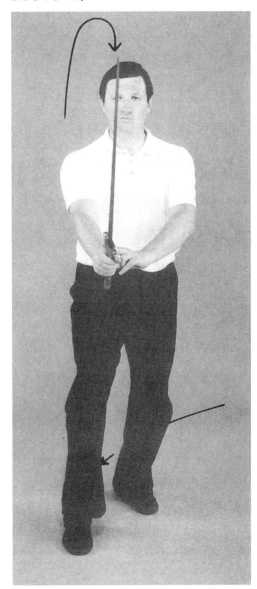

Fig. 319 *(Chop down)* Turn your right foot in and shift your weight on to your right foot. Rotate your body to the left and turn out your left foot. Take one step towards the north as you circle the sword over your head and chop down to the north.

Move 48

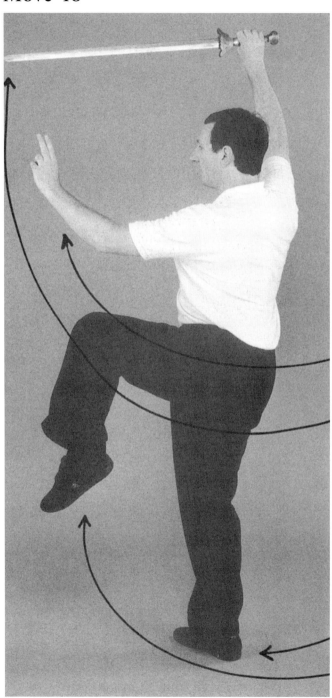

Fig. 320 *(Big dipper)* Take one step towards the east with your right foot. As you turn your body to the east, lift up your left knee and sweep up the sword. The left hand is positioned under the sword as before.

Move 49

Fig. 321 *(Scoop down and chop)* Place your left foot forwards half a step to the east and scoop down the sword to the west. Take one step forwards with your right foot and continue the circle. Chop with the back of the sword to the east as you swing your left arm out.

Move 50

Fig. 322 *(Hold the moon)* Shift your weight back on to your left foot, in a cat stance, as you pull the sword back with both hands near to your stomach.

Move 51

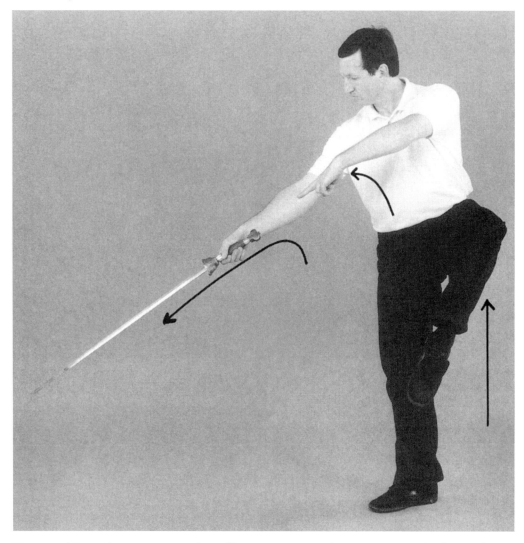

Fig. 323 *(Green dragon jumps in the well)* Move your weight on to your right foot and thrust the sword down at a 45° angle, moving your left hand up behind and in line with the sword hilt. The left foot is raised.

Move 52

Fig. 324 Shift your weight back on to your left foot and sweep the sword back past your left ear.

Move 53

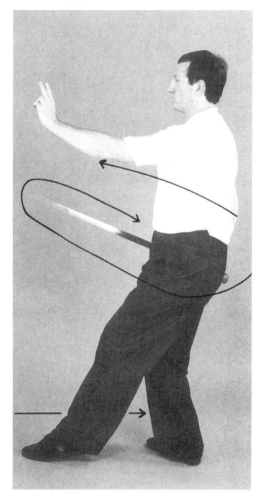

Fig. 325 *(Shoot the wild goose)* Step back with your right foot to the west and continue to sweep the sword down to the east and back near the hip. As the sword pulls back to the hip, point your left fingers to the east.

Move 54

Fig. 326 *(A compass point)* Take one step forwards with your right foot parallel with your left, the feet one shoulder width wide. As you do this, thrust your sword directly forwards to the east.

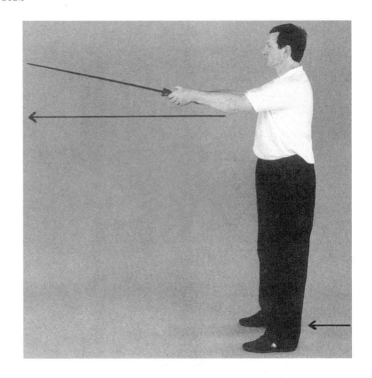

Move 55

Fig. 327 *(Phoenix spreads its wings)* Bend your knees, swing your right foot to the north-west, turn your body to the right and sweep with the sword as in move 21.

Move 56

Fig. 328 *(Intercept to the left)* Shift your weight on to your right foot and circle your left leg one step towards the north. Rotate your body to the left, shifting your weight on to your left leg, and sweep the sword in front of you.

Move 57

Fig. 329 Step forwards with your right foot as you continue to sweep the sword to the left and then the right, finishing near your right knee.

Move 58

Fig. 330 *(Shoot the wild goose)* Step forwards with your left leg towards the east.

Move 59

Fig. 331 *(A compass point)* Move your right leg up to your left leg and repeat move 54. To the east.

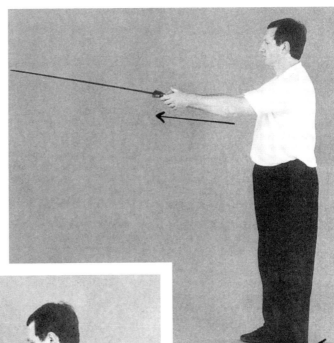

Move 60

Fig. 332 *(Fall down like plum blossoms right)* Take one step back to the west with your right foot and pull the sword back near to your right hip, with your left fingers touching the right wrist. Your right hand is facing down.

Move 61

Fig. 333 *(Fall down like plum blossoms left)* Move your left foot one step back towards the west. As you do so, sweep the sword in front of you, ending near your left hip.

Move 62

Fig. 334 *(Fall down like plum blossoms right)* Step back with your right toot towards the west and repeat move 60.

Move 63

Fig. 335 *(Fall down like plum blossoms left)* Step back with your left foot to the west and repeat move 61.

Move 64

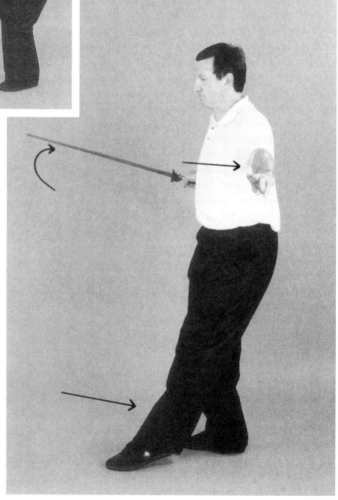

Fig. 336 Step back with your right foot and separate your right and left hands to the sides.

Move 65

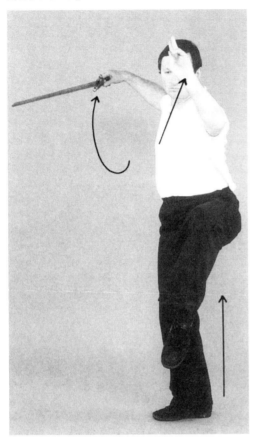

Fig. 337 Lift your sword up with the point slightly down and turn to the north. At the same time, lift up your left arm and leg.

Move 66

Fig. 338 Take one step forwards towards the north, thrusting the sword down and raising your left arm.

Move 67

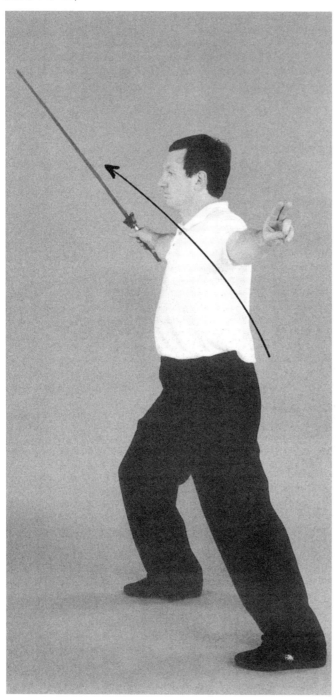

Fig. 339 *(Tiger lifts its tail)*
Circle the sword up and to
the right, with the sword
held vertically. As you
move the sword across, you
should turn your body to
the right.

Move 68

Fig. 340 *(Fish leaps from the river)* Lift your right knee and move the sword into the centre as your left hand holds the right hand.

Move 69

Repeat move 15. To the east.

Move 70

Repeat move 16. To the east.

Move 71

Fig. 341 Repeat move 17. To the east.

Move 72

Fig. 342 *(Black dragon wraps around pillar)* Shift your weight on to your left leg. Turn your body to the left while moving the sword to your left shoulder. As you turn the body, your left fingers touch the right wrist.

Move 73

Fig. 343 Turn the right foot out, pivot your body to the right and swing your left foot to the east. As you do this, circle the sword near your right shoulder.

Move 74

Fig. 344 *(Sage points the way)* Step forwards with your right foot, separate your left hand near to your temple and thrust your sword to the east.

Move 75

Fig. 345 *(Offer the sword)* Shift your weight on to your left leg in a snake stance. As you turn your body to the left, move the sword to the left shoulder and touch the right wrist with the left fingers.

Move 76

Fig. 346 *(Wind blows the plum blossoms)* Shift your weight on to your right foot, moving the sword vertically to the right.

Move 77

Fig. 347 Move your left hand to the left.

Move 78

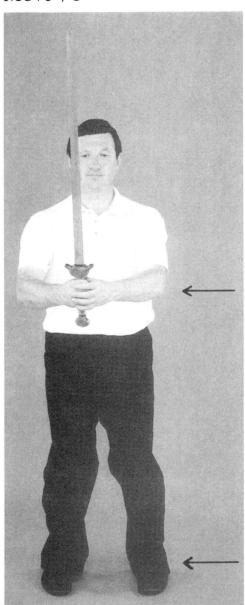

Fig. 348 Move your left foot in, near to the right, and move your right hand to the west while taking your left hand across to hold the sword.

Move 79

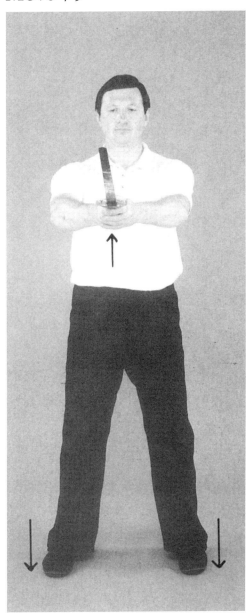

Fig. 349 *(A compass point)* Step forwards with your right foot, followed by the left, and thrust the sword forwards as before, to the north.

Move 80

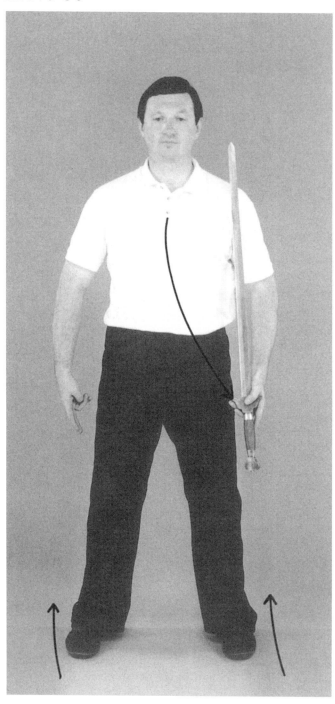

Fig. 350 *(Finish)* Step back with your left foot and then your right and move the sword to your shoulder.

Index